THE WHEEL

The Wheel

An Anthology of Religious Verse

Compiled by

EMMELINE GARNETT

LONDON
BURNS & OATES
MACMILLAN & CO LTD
1965

Introduction

THERE are two wheels. One is the cycle of the church year, from the first Sunday in Advent to the last after Pentecost or Trinity, and the other is the cycle of the old mystery plays, which began with Creation and ended with the Day of Judgment. The cycle of the natural year fits in too, from the sad, dying days of autumn, through the darkness of winter, into the light and growth of spring, and round again to the harvest.

I

The wheel begins, as the old miracle plays began, with the wonder of God the Creator and his creation, through the traditional steps of the Genesis story, to the making of man.

II

Man, at first in a paradise of innocence, falls into sin and so knows evil and death, but neither his ejection from the garden, nor death, prove to be so very terrible. They are the beginning rather than the end of things.

III

Through the 'four thousand winters' of the Old Testament, and in his own darkness, man waits, struggling always hopefully to find his God.

IV

The waiting draws to an end, and the promises become clearer and clearer. The world is waiting for the Messiah, Mary most eagerly of all.

V

He comes, on Christmas night, a light in the dark days of midwinter.

VI

The door is opened. The New Year follows, and the other traditional feasts of the Twelve Days of Christmas.

VII

Now we must follow Christ into his life and our own, the 'kingdom of anxiety'. We find him in all the ordinary working days of a twentieth-century civilisation.

VIII

We seek and sorrow after him through our own sin and darkness, epitomised by the long sad days of Lent.

IX

Lent is followed inexorably by Holy Week, by the short-lived triumph of Palm Sunday, and then by Calvary and crucifixion.

X

Christ rises from the dead, as the winter world springs to life again, and man is reborn through baptism. This is the triple theme of resurrection.

XI

In the summer feasts of Pentecost and Corpus Christi, the theme is love, God's love for us, and ours for each other in the corporate life of the Christian church.

XII

In the end is the beginning. The wheel comes full circle — the year is fulfilled in the harvest, and man is fulfilled in his death and in his contemplation of the future after death.

Contents

vii

III. FOUR THOUSAND WINTERS

IV. COMFORT YE MY PEOPLE

V. CHRISTMAS EVE AND TWELVE OF THE CLOCK

VI. AND LET THE NEW YEAR IN

VII. SEEK HIM IN THE KINGDOM OF ANXIETY

X. DEATH AND DARKNESS, GET YOU PACKING

XI. THE SPIRIT IS RUNNING, THE DARKNESS IS ENDING

XII. AND THE CITY WAS PURE GOLD

Acknowledgments

THE editor and publishers wish to acknowledge their indebtedness to the following, who have kindly given permission for the use of copyright material:

Mrs. George Bambridge and Messrs. Methuen & Co., Ltd., for lines from 'M'Andrew's Hymn', from *The Seven Seas*, by Rudyard Kipling; Miss Edith C. Batho, for her translations of the Spanish ballads 'St. Joseph and God's Mother' and 'As Mary was a-walking'; the Estate of Hilaire Belloc, for 'Is there any reward?', from *Verse*, by Hilaire Belloc; Mr. Thomas Blackburn, for 'The Spirit Dances'; Mr. John Blackie and Messrs. Basil Blackwell & Mott, Ltd., for 'Space Pilot', from *Mystery, Magic and Adventure*; The Bodley Head, Ltd., for 'To the Sun', from *The Collected Poems of Roy Campbell*; the Executors of the Roy Campbell Estate and Messrs. Jonathan Cape, Ltd., for the lines from 'The Flaming Terrapin'; the Executors of the Roy Campbell Estate, for 'The Theology of Bongwi, the Baboon', from *Adamastor*; Messrs. Jonathan Cape, Ltd., for 'Cabbages', by Teresa Hooley, and 'The Christmas Tree' and 'Now the Full-throated Daffodils', by C. Day Lewis; Messrs. Jonathan Cape, Ltd., and Holt, Rinehart & Winston, Inc., for three poems from *Chicago Poems*, by Carl Sandburg, Copyright 1916 by Holt, Rinehart & Winston, Inc., Copyright renewed 1944 by Carl Sandburg; Mr. Charles Causley and Messrs. Rupert Hart-Davis, Ltd., for the envoi, here called 'I am the Prince', to 'Ballad of the Five Continents', and 'I am the Great Sun', from *Union Street*; The Clarendon Press, Oxford, for 'The Happy Land' and the extract from 'The Dream of the Rood', from *Anglo-Saxon Poetry*, translated by Gavin Bone; Miss D. E. Collins, for 'A Christmas Carol', by G. K. Chesterton; Messrs. Constable & Co., Ltd., for the extracts from *Mediaeval Latin Lyrics*, translated by Helen Waddell; the Literary Trustees of Walter de la Mare and The Society of

Authors as their representative, for 'All but Blind';
Messrs. J. M. Dent & Sons, Ltd., for the lines from
Everyman, a miracle play; Messrs. André Deutsch, Ltd.,
for 'The Annunciation', from *A Sense of the World*, by
Elizabeth Jennings; Evans Plays, for three extracts from
Wakefield Mystery Plays, edited by Martial Rose; Messrs.
Faber & Faber, Ltd., for the extract from 'Sext', No. 3
from 'Horae Canonicae', from *The Shield of Achilles*, and
lines from 'The Flight into Egypt', from *For the Time
Being*, by W. H. Auden, and 'Journey of the Magi', from
Collected Poems, and 'Little Gidding', Part IV, from *Four
Quartets*, by T. S. Eliot; Mr. Monk Gibbon, for 'French
Peasants', from *For Daws to Peck At*; Harper & Row,
Publishers, Inc., for 'Simon the Cyrenian Speaks', from
Color, by Countee Cullen; The Trustees of the Hardy
Estate, for 'The Oxen', from *The Collected Poems of Thomas
Hardy*; Messrs. Rupert Hart-Davis, Ltd., for 'Cynddylan
on a Tractor', from *Song at the Year's Turning*, by R. S.
Thomas; Miss Phyllis Hartnoll, for 'Bethlehem', 'The
Carpenter' and 'Twelfth Night'; Heinemann Educational
Books, Ltd., for 'Abraham and Isaac' and 'Adoration of the
Shepherds', translated by Maurice Hussey; International
Authors N.V., the owners of Mr. Robert Graves's
copyrights, for 'In the Wilderness', from *Collected Poems*;
The Macmillan Company, New York, for 'Daniel', from
Collected Poems by Vachel Lindsay. Copyright 1920 by The
Macmillan Company, Renewed 1948 by Elizabeth C.
Lindsay, and for 'General William Booth Enters into
Heaven', from *Collected Poems* by Vachel Lindsay. Copy-
right 1913 by The Macmillan Company; Messrs. Hughes
Massie, Ltd., for the extract from 'Songs between the Soul
and the Bridegroom', from *Poems of St. John of the Cross*,
translated by Roy Campbell; Father Brian Moore, S.J., for
'Veni Creator' and 'Veni Sancte Spiritus'; New Directions,
for the lines from 'An Argument — of the Passion of

Christ', from *A Man in the Divided Sea*, by Thomas Merton; Messrs. Oliver & Boyd, Ltd., for 'Hey The Gift Ho the Gift' and 'Charm', from *Carmina Gadelica*, translated by Alexander Carmichael; the Oxford University Press, for 'The Sun that Warms You' and 'Libra', from *Children's Bells*, by Eleanor Farjeon, and 'Pied Beauty', 'Easter' and the lines from 'S. Thomae Aquinatis', here called, 'Godhead here in Hiding', by Gerard Manley Hopkins; the Oxford University Press, Music Department, for 'Come and I will sing to you' and 'The Cherry Tree Carol', from *English Folk Songs from the Southern Appalachians*, compiled by Cecil Sharp.

Pegasus Press, Ltd., for 'On the Swag', by R. A. K. Mason; Penguin Books, Ltd., for 'Confession', from *Il Purgatorio*, by Dorothy L. Sayers; Messrs. Laurence Pollinger, Ltd., the Estate of the late Mrs. Frieda Lawrence, and Messrs. William Heinemann, Ltd., for four poems from *The Complete Poems of D. H. Lawrence* and an extract from *The Rainbow*, by D. H. Lawrence; Mr. Ezra Pound, for 'Meditatio'; Messrs. Routledge & Kegan Paul, Ltd., for 'St. John the Baptist', from *Collected Poems*, by Sidney Keyes; Mr. Clive Sansom and Messrs. Methuen & Co., Ltd., for 'Mary of Nazareth', 'Martha of Bethany' and 'The Donkey's Owner', from *The Witnesses and Other Poems*, and the lines from *The Cathedral*; Mr. Siegfried Sassoon, for 'Everyone Sang' and 'A Flower has Opened'; Messrs. Martin Secker & Warburg, Ltd., for the two verses from the Epilogue to 'The Golden Journey to Samarkand', by James Elroy Flecker; Messrs. Sheed & Ward, Ltd., for the extracts from *Piers Plowman*, translated by H. W. Wells, and the extracts from poems from *The Flowering Tree*, by Caryll Houselander; the author's representatives and Messrs. Sidgwick & Jackson, Ltd., for the extract from 'Heaven', from *The Collected Poems of Rupert Brooke*; Dame Edith Sitwell, for 'Still Falls the

Rain', from *Collected Poems*; The Society for Promoting Christian Knowledge, for 'The Scriveners' Play', from *The York Cycle of Mystery Plays*, edited by Dr. J. S. Purvis; the Trustees of the Tagore Estate for no. XC from 'Gitanjali' from the *Collected Poems and Plays of Rabindranath Tagore*, and for the poem on page 126, here called 'A Song of Kabir', from *One Hundred Poems of Kabir*, and for the poem on page 151, here called 'The Conqueror'; Messrs. Thames and Hudson, Ltd., for 'To the Nativity', by Fernán González de Eslava, and 'Sonnet', by Miguel de Guevara, from *An Anthology of Mexican Poetry*, translated by Samuel Beckett; and The Viking Press, Inc., for 'The Creation', from *God's Trombones*, by James Weldon Johnson, Copyright 1927 by The Viking Press, Inc., 1954, by Grace Nail Johnson.

'The cycle of creation still wheeled in the Church year. . . . So the children lived the year of Christianity, the epic of the soul of mankind. Year by year the inner, unknown drama went on in them, their hearts were born and came to fulness, suffered on the cross, gave up the ghost, and rose again to unnumbered days, untired, having at least this rhythm of eternity in a ragged, inconsequential life.'

D. H. LAWRENCE *The Rainbow*

I

One
O
one
was
God
alone

O WORSHIP THE KING

O worship the king
All glorious above!
O gratefully sing
His power and his love;
Our shield and defender,
The ancient of days,
Pavilioned in splendour,
And girded with praise.

O tell of his might,
O sing of his grace,
Whose robe is the light,
Whose canopy space.
His chariots of wrath
The deep thunder clouds form,
And dark is his path
On the wings of the storm.

Sir Robert Grant

From 'The Flaming Terrapin'

From the blue vault, with rosy glow
    In shimmering descent,
Ten thousand angels fell like snow,
Ten thousand tumbling angels went
Careering on the winds, and hurled
Their rainbow-lazos to pursue
    The wild, unbroken world!
Saddled on shooting stars they flew
And rode them down with manes aflare,
Stampeding with a wild halloo,
Gymnastic on the rushing air.

3

Down on the hills, with a shatter of flame,
The topsy-turvy horsemen came,
The angel cowboys, flaring white,
With lariats twirling, cracking whips,
And long hair foaming in the light,
Vaulting on the saw-backed ridges
Where they tear the sky to strips,
And the rack of thunder bridges
Mountain-tops in dense eclipse. . . .

Roy Campbell

MICHAEL, ARCHANGEL

Michael, Archangel
Of the King of Kings,
Give ear to our voices.

Thou wert seen in the Temple of God,
A censer of gold in thy hands,
And the smoke of it fragrant with spices
Rose up till it came before God.

Thou with strong hand didst smite the cruel dragon,
And many souls didst rescue from his jaws.
Then was there a great silence in heaven,
And a thousand thousand saying 'Glory to the Lord King'.

Hear us, Michael,
Greatest angel,
Come down a little
From thy high seat,
To bring us the strength of God
And the lightening of His mercy.

4

And do thou, Gabriel,
Lay low our foes,
And thou, Raphael,
Heal our sick,
Purge our disease, ease thou our pain,
And give us to share
In the joys of the blessed.

Alcuin, translated by Helen Waddell

ANGELS
from 'The Faerie Queene', Book II

And is there care in heaven? And is there love
   In heavenly spirits to these creatures base
   That may compassion of their evils move?
   There is, else much more wretched were the case
   Of men than beasts. But O the exceeding grace
   Of highest God, that loves his creatures so,
   And all his works with mercy doth embrace,
   That blessed angels he sends to and fro
To serve to wicked man, to serve his wicked foe.

How oft do they their silver bowers leave,
   To come to succour us that succour want?
   How oft do they with golden pinions cleave
   The flitting skies, like flying pursuivant,
   Against foul fiends to aid us militant?
   They for us fight, they watch and duly ward
   And their bright squadrons round about us plant,
   And all for love, and nothing for reward.
O why should heavenly God to men have such regard?

Edmund Spenser

5

ETERNITY

I saw Eternity the other night
Like a great ring of pure and endless light,
      All calm, as it was bright;
And round beneath it, Time in hours, days, years
      Driven by the spheres
Like a vast shadow moved, in which the world
      And all her train were hurled.

Henry Vaughan

CREATOR

God moves in a mysterious way
His wonders to perform,
He plants his footsteps in the sea
And rides upon the storm.

Deep in unfathomable mines
Of never-failing skill
He treasures up his bright designs
And works his sovereign will.

William Cowper

THE CREATION

And God stepped out on space,
And he looked around and said:
I'm lonely —
I'll make me a world.

As far as the eye of God could see
Darkness covered everything,

6

Blacker than a hundred midnights
Down in a cypress swamp.

Then God smiled,
And the light broke,
And the darkness rolled up on one side,
And the light stood shining on the other,
And God said : That's good!

Then God reached out and took the light in his hands,
And God rolled the light around in his hands
Until he made the sun;
And he set that sun a-blazing in the heavens.
And the light that was left from making the sun
God gathered it up in a shining ball
And flung it against the darkness,
Spangling the night with the moon and stars.
Then down between
The darkness and the light
He hurled the world;
And God said : That's good!

Then God himself stepped down —
And the sun was on his right hand,
And the moon was on his left;
The stars were clustered about his head,
And the earth was under his feet.
And God walked, and where he trod
His footsteps hollowed the valleys out
And bulged the mountains up.

Then he stopped and looked and saw
That the earth was hot and barren.
So God stepped over to the edge of the world

And he spat out the seven seas —
He batted his eyes, and the lightnings flashed —
He clapped his hands, and the thunders rolled —
And the waters above the earth came down,
The cooling waters came down.

Then the green grass sprouted,
And the little red flowers blossomed,
The pine tree pointed his finger to the sky,
And the oak spread out his arms,
The lakes cuddled down in the hollows of the ground,
And the rivers ran down to the sea;
And God smiled again,
And the rainbow appeared
And curled itself around his shoulder.

Then God raised his arm and he waved his hand
Over the sea and over the land,
And he said : Bring forth! Bring forth!
And quicker than God could drop his hand,
Fishes and fowls
And beasts and birds
Swam the rivers and the seas,
Roamed the forests and the woods,
And split the air with their wings.
And God said : That's good!

Then God walked around,
And God looked around
On all that he had made.
He looked at his sun,
And he looked at his moon,
And he looked at his little stars;
He looked on his world

With all its living things,
And God said : I'm lonely still.

Then God sat down —
On the side of a hill where he could think;
By a deep, wide river he sat down;
With his head in his hands,
God thought and thought,
Till he thought, I'll make me a man!

Up from the bed of the river
God scooped the clay;
And by the bank of the river
He kneeled him down;
And there the great God Almighty
Who lit the sun and fixed it in the sky,
Who flung the stars to the most far corner of the night,
Who rounded the earth in the middle of his hand;
This Great God,
Like a mammy bending over her baby,
Kneeled down in the dust
Toiling over a lump of clay
Till he shaped it in his own image;
Then into it he blew the breath of life,
And man became a living soul.
Amen. Amen.

James Weldon Johnson

HAPPY THOUGHT

The world is so full of a number of things,
I'm sure we should all be as happy as kings.

Robert Louis Stevenson

RED GERANIUM AND
GODLY MIGNONETTE

Imagine that any mind ever *thought* a red geranium!
As if the redness of a red geranium could be anything but
 a sensual experience
and as if sensual experience could take place before there
 were any senses.
We know that even God could not imagine the redness of a
 red geranium
nor the smell of mignonette
when geraniums were not, and mignonette neither.
And even when they were, even God would have to have a
 nose to smell at the mignonette.
You can't imagine the Holy Ghost sniffing at cherry-pie
 heliotrope.
Or the Most High, during the coal age, cudgelling his
 mighty brains
even if he had any brains : straining his mighty mind
to think, among the moss and mud of lizards and mastodons
to think out, in the abstract, when all was twilit green and
 muddy :
'Now there shall be tum-tiddly-um, and tum-tiddly-um,
hey-presto! scarlet geranium!'

We know it couldn't be done.
But imagine, among the mud and the mastodons
god sighing and yearning with tremendous creative
 yearning, in that dark green mess
oh, for some other beauty, some other beauty
that blossomed at last, red geranium, and mignonette.

D. H. Lawrence

10

CABBAGES

If God were as ungenerous as man,
He would make cabbages, to feed the kine,
On some unbeautiful and heavy plan,
Meet for mere beasts. But in His craft divine
He fashions them, and colours them instead
With gold and misty blue amid the green,
Softly with purple, gallantly with red.
He curves their leaves and traces veins between;
Bejewels them with drops of rain and dew;
Caresses them with wind, and, crowning boon,
With lunar light transfigures them anew —
Great silver roses 'neath the autumn moon.

Teresa Hooley

TWO LIMERICKS

There was a young man who said 'God
Must find it remarkably odd
    That this sycamore tree
    Continues to be
When there's no one about in the quad.'

'Dear Sir — I do not find it odd,
Though there's no one about in the quad,
    That the sycamore tree
    Continues to be,
Since observed by — Yours faithfully — God.'

Anonymous

TIGER

Tiger! Tiger! burning bright
In the forests of the night,
What immortal hand or eye
Could frame thy fearful symmetry?

In what distant deeps or skies
Burnt the fire of thine eyes?
On what wings dare he aspire?
What the hand dare seize the fire?

And what shoulder, and what art
Could twist the sinews of thy heart?
And when thy heart began to beat,
What dread hand? and what dread feet?

What the hammer? What the chain?
In what furnace was thy brain?
What the anvil? What dread grasp
Dare its deadly terrors clasp?

When the stars threw down their spears
And watered heaven with their tears,
Did he smile his work to see?
Did he who made the lamb make thee?

Tiger! Tiger! burning bright
In the forests of the night,
What immortal hand or eye
Dare frame thy fearful symmetry?

William Blake

THE MARVEL OF BIRDS
from 'Piers Plowman', Passus XI

I saw bushes where birds build for nesting.
No one has the wit to work so rarely.
I wondered from whom and where the magpie
Had learned to lay the sticks on which she lies for breeding.
No carpenter could have constructed that cage for wages.
If a mason should make a mould for it there were much to
    wonder at.

Yet I marvelled more how many wild fowl
Conceal and cover their eggs so closely,
On moors and on marshes, that men may not find them,
And hide their eggs whenever they leave them,
Lest wild animals and hawks should know it.
Some tread their mates and breed in the branches
And bring forth the young birds above all danger. . . .
I marvelled much what master taught them,
And who taught them to timber in the trees so boldly,
Where no man nor beast may reach them nesting.

       William Langland, translated by H. W. Wells

MAN
from 'Hamlet'

What a piece of work is a man, how noble in reason, how
infinite in faculties, in form and moving how express and
admirable, in action how like an angel, in apprehension
how like a god : the beauty of the world : the paragon of
animals.

           William Shakespeare

PERSONALITY

(Musings of a Police Reporter in the Identification Bureau)

You have loved forty women, but you have only one thumb.

You have led a hundred secret lives, but you mark only one thumb.

You go round the world and fight in a thousand wars and win all the world's honours, but when you come back home the print of the one thumb your mother gave you is the same print of thumb you had in the old home when your mother kissed you and said goodbye.

From the whirling womb of time come millions of men and their feet crowd the earth and they cut one another's throats for room to stand and among them all are not two thumbs alike.

Somewhere is a Great God of Thumbs who can tell the inside story of this.

Carl Sandburg

ALL PEOPLE THAT ON EARTH DO DWELL

All people that on earth do dwell
Sing to the Lord with cheerful voice;
Him serve with fear, his praise forth tell,
Come ye before him, and rejoice.

The Lord, ye know, is God indeed;
Without our aid he did us make;
We are his folk, he doth us feed,
And for his sheep he doth us take.

William Kethe

MIRACLES

Why, who makes much of a miracle?
As to me I know of nothing else but miracles,
Whether I walk the streets of Manhattan,
Or dart my sight over the roofs of houses toward the sky,
Or wade with naked feet along the beach just in the edge of
     the water,
Or stand under trees in the woods,
Or talk by day with any one I love, or sleep in the bed at
     night with any one I love,
Or sit at table at dinner with the rest,
Or look at strangers opposite me riding in the car,
Or watch honey-bees busy round the hive of a summer
     forenoon,
Or animals feeding in the fields,
Or birds, or the wonderfulness of insects in the air,
Or the wonderfulness of the sundown, or of stars shining so
     quiet and bright,
Or the exquisite delicate thin curve of the new moon in
     spring;
These with the rest, one and all, are to me miracles,
The whole referring, yet each distinct and in its place.

To me every hour of the light and dark is a miracle,
Every cubic inch of space is a miracle,
Every square yard of the surface of the earth is spread with
     the same,
Every foot of the interior swarms with the same,
To me the sun is a continual miracle,
The fishes that swim — the rocks — the motion of the
     waves — the ships with men in them,
What stranger miracles are there?

Walt Whitman

PIED BEAUTY

Glory be to God for dappled things —
   For skies of couple-colour as a brinded cow;
     For rose-moles all in stipple upon trout that swim;
Fresh-firecoal chestnut-falls; finches' wings;
   Landscape plotted and pieced — fold, fallow, and plough;
     And all trades, their gear and tackle and trim.

All things counter, original, spare, strange;
   Whatever is fickle, freckled (who knows how?)
     With swift, slow; sweet, sour; adazzle, dim;
He fathers-forth whose beauty is past change:
     Praise him.

Gerard Manley Hopkins

COME AND I WILL SING YOU

Come and I will sing you.
   What will you sing me?
I will sing you one.
   What is your one?
One O one was God alone and he shall ever remain so.

Come and I will sing you.
   What will you sing me?
I will sing you two.
   What is your two?
Two O two are the lily-white babes clothed in darling
   green O,
One O one was God alone and he shall ever remain so.

Come and I will sing you.
   What will you sing me?

16

I will sing you three.
What is your three?

Three of them are strangers,
Two O two are the lily-white babes clothed in darling
green O,
One O one was God alone and he shall ever remain so.

Come and I will sing you.
What will you sing me?
I will sing you four.
What is your four?

Four are the gospel preachers,
Three of them are strangers,
Two O two are the lily-white babes clothed in darling
green O,
One O one was God alone and he shall ever remain so.

(*And so on up to twelve. The last verse runs as follows:*)
Twelve are the twelve apostles,
Eleven are the eleven who went to heaven,
Ten are the ten commandments,
Nine are the nine that dress so fine,
Eight are the great archangels,
Seven are the seven stars fixed in the sky,
Six are the cheerful waiters,
Five are the farmers in a boat,
Four are the gospel preachers,
Three of them are strangers,
Two O two are the lily-white babes clothed in darling
green O,
One O one was God alone and he shall ever remain so.

Anonymous. Appalachian Folk Song

PRAISE YE THE LORD
from the Authorised Version of the Bible

Praise ye the Lord. Praise God in his sanctuary : praise him
in the firmament of his power.

Praise him for his mighty acts : praise him according to his
excellent greatness.

Praise him with the sound of the trumpet : praise him with
the psaltery and harp.

Praise him with the timbrel and dance : praise him with
stringed instruments and organs.

Praise him upon the loud cymbals : praise him upon the
high sounding cymbals.

Let everything that hath breath praise the Lord. Praise ye
the Lord.

Psalm 150

II

Lonesome Valley

THE HAPPY LAND
from 'The Phoenix'

I have heard there is hence
Far away from the world
A nook in the East, a noble plain,
Great, and girt with gallant trees,
Which the Lord from living men
Has shut tight, shielded quite,
Since he formed first the world.
That victorious plain pleasant shall remain,
With no pain and no rain,
No showers to steep, no rime to creep,
No hot sky, no screaming hail;
Always the plain is a pleasant place.
For there are no mountains high and proud,
Nor any stone cliffs, starving clefts,
Precipices leaning up, precipices leaning down,
But the noble plain never fails to stand
Even and open, unanxiously perfect.
That bright bower does bravely tower
Ten times as high as the tallest hill,
Which white and bright gives the world light
And shines to men under the shining of the stars.
    Anonymous. Anglo-Saxon, translated by Gavin Bone

INNOCENCE

How like an angel came I down!
How bright are all things here!
When first among his works I did appear
O how their glory me did crown!
The world resembled his eternity,
In which my soul did walk;

And every thing that I did see
    Did with me talk.

The skies in their magnificence,
    The lively, lovely air,
O how divine, how soft, how sweet, how fair!
    The stars did entertain my sense,
And all the works of God so bright and pure,
      So rich and great did seem,
    As if they ever must endure,
      In my esteem.

A native health and innocence
    Within my bones did grow,
And while my God did all his glories show,
    I felt a vigour in my sense
That was all spirit. I within did flow
      With seas of life, like wine;
    I nothing in the world did know
      But 'twas divine.

Thomas Traherne

THOUGHTS IN A GARDEN

Fair Quiet, have I found thee here,
And innocence thy sister dear!
Mistaken long, I sought you then
In busy companies of men.
Your sacred plants, if here below,
Only among the plants will grow.
Society is all but rude,
To this delicious solitude. . . .

What wondrous life is this I lead!
Ripe apples drop about my head;
The luscious clusters of the vine
Upon my mouth do crush their wine;
The nectarine and curious peach
Into my hands themselves do reach;
Stumbling on melons, as I pass
Ensnared with flowers, I fall on grass.

Here, at the fountain's sliding foot,
Or at some fruit-tree's mossy root,
Casting the body's vest aside,
My soul into the boughs does glide;
There like a bird it sits and sings,
Then whets, and combs its silver wings;
And, till prepared for longer flight,
Waves in its plumes the various light.

Such was that happy garden-state
While man there walked without a mate:
After a place so pure and sweet,
What other help could yet be meet!
But 'twas beyond a mortal's share
To wander solitary there:
Two paradises 'twere in one
To live in Paradise alone.

Andrew Marvell

EVIL

Evil no nature hath; the loss of good
Is that which gives to sin a livelihood.

Robert Herrick

THESE BONES GWINE TO RISE AGIN

Lord, he thought he'd make a man,
>   (*These bones gwine to rise agin*)
Made him out of mud an' a little bit of sand,
>   (*These bones gwine to rise agin*)
>   *I know it, 'deed I know it,*
>   *These bones gwine to rise agin.*

Adam was the first he made,
He put him on the bank and lay him in the shade.

Thought he'd make a woman too —
Didn't know 'xactly what to do.

Took a rib from Adam's side —
Made Miss' Eve to be his bride.

Put 'em in a garden rich an' fair,
Tol' 'em they might eat whatever was there.

But to one tree they mus' not go —
Mus' leave the apples there to grow.

Ol' Miss Eve come walkin' roun',
Spied a tree all loaded down.

Serpent quoiled aroun' the trunk,
At Miss' Eve his eye he wunk.

Firs' she took a little pull,
Then she filled her apron full.

24

Then Adam took a little slice,
Smack his lips an' say 'twas nice.

The Lord he come a-wanderin' roun',
Spied them peelin's on the groun'.

The Lord he speak with a monstrous voice —
Shuck this ol' world to its very joists.

'Adam, Adam, where art thou?'
'Here, Mass' Lord, I'se a-comin' now.'

'Stole my apples, I believe?'
'No, Mass' Lord, but I spec' it was Eve.'

The Lord he ris' up in his wrath,
Tol' 'em, 'You beat it down the path'.

'Out of this garden you must git —
Earn yo' livin' by yo' sweat.'

He put an angel at the door,
Tol' em not to come there never no more.

Of this apple there ain' no more —
                    (*These bones gwine to rise agin*)
Eve ate the apple, give Adam the core.
                    (*These bones gwine to rise agin*)
                    I know it, 'deed I know it,
                    These bones gwine to rise agin.

Anonymous. American Folk Song

ONLY MAN

Only man can fall from God
Only man.
No animal, no beast nor creeping thing
no cobra nor hyena nor scorpion nor hideous white ant
can slip entirely through the fingers of the hands of god
into the abyss of self-knowledge,
knowledge of the self-apart-from-god.

For the knowledge of the self-apart-from-god
is an abyss down which the soul can slip
writhing and twisting in all the revolutions
of the unfinished plunge
of self-awareness, now apart from God, falling
fathomless, fathomless, self-consciousness wriggling
writhing deeper and deeper in all the minutiae of self-
        knowledge,
downwards, exhaustive,
yet never, never coming to the bottom, for there is no
        bottom;
zigzagging down like the fizzle from a finished rocket
the frizzling falling fire that cannot go out, dropping
        wearily,
neither can it reach the depth
for the depth is bottomless,
so it wriggles its way ever further down, further down
at last in sheer horror of not being able to leave off
knowing itself, knowing itself apart from God, falling.

                                        D. H. Lawrence

DUESSA'S COACH
from 'The Faerie Queene', Book I

But this was drawn of six unequal beasts
   On which her six sage counsellors did ride,
   Taught to obey their bestial behests,
   With like conditions to their kinds applied :
   Of which the first, that all the rest did guide,
   Was sluggish *Idleness*, the nurse of sin;
   Upon a slothful ass he chose to ride,
   Arrayed in habit black and amice thin,
Like to a holy monk, the service to begin. . . .

And by his side rode loathsome *Gluttony*,
   Deformed creature, on a filthy swine,
   His belly was up-blown with luxury,
   And eke with fatness swollen were his eyne,
   And like a crane his neck was long and fine,
   With which he swallowed up excessive feast,
   For want of which poor people oft did pine;
   And all the way, most like a brutish beast,
He spewed up his gorge, that all did him detest. . . .

And next to him rode lustful *Lechery*,
   Upon a bearded goat, whose rugged hair,
   And whally eyes (the sign of jealousy)
   Was like the person self, whom he did bear :
   Who rough, and black, and filthy did appear,
   Unseemly man to please fair lady's eye,
   Yet he of ladies oft was loved dear,
   When fairer faces were bid standen by :
O who does know the bent of women's fantasy ? . . .

And greedy *Avarice* by him did ride,
    Upon a camel loaded all with gold;
    Two iron coffers hung on either side,
    With precious metal full as they might hold,
    And in his lap a heap of coin he told;
    For of his wicked pelf his God he made,
    And into hell himself for money sold;
    Accursed usury was all his trade,
And right and wrong alike in equal balance weighed. . . .

And next to him malicious *Envy* rode
    Upon a ravenous wolf, that still did chaw
    Between his cankered teeth a venemous toad,
    That all the poison ran about his jaw;
    But inwardly he chewed his own maw
    At neighbour's wealth, that made him ever sad;
    For death it was, when any good he saw.
    And wept, that cause of weeping none he had,
But when he heard of harm, he waxed wondrous glad. . . .

And him beside rides fierce revenging *Wrath*,
    Upon a lion, loth for to be led;
    And in his hand a burning brand he hath
    The which he brandishes about his head;
    His eyes did hurl forth sparkles fiery red,
    And stared stern on all, that him beheld,
    As ashes pale of hue and seeming dead;
    And on his dagger still his hand he held,
Trembling through hasty rage, when choler in him
    swelled. . . .

And after all, upon the wagon beam
    Rode *Satan*, with a smarting whip in hand,
    With which he forward lashed the lazy team,
    So oft as *Sloth* still in the mire did stand.

Huge routs of people did about them band,
Shouting for joy, and still before their way
A foggy mist had covered all the land;
And underneath their feet, all scattered lay
Dead skulls and bones of men, whose life had gone astray.

Edmund Spenser

DEATH
from 'Paradise Lost', Book XII

Adam speaks:
'Alas, both for the deed and for the cause!
But have I now seen Death? Is this the way
I must return to native dust? O sight
Of terror, foul and ugly to behold,
Horrid to think, how horrible to feel!'
To whom thus Michael: 'Death thou hast seen
In his first shape on man; but many shapes
Of Death, and many are the ways that lead
To his grim cave, all dismal; yet to sense
More terrible at the entrance than within.
Some, as thou sawest, by violent stroke shall die,
By fire, flood, famine, by intemperance more
In meats and drinks, which on the earth shall bring
Diseases dire, of which a monstrous crew
Before thee shall appear; that thou mayst know
What misery the inabstinence of Eve
Shall bring on men.' Immediately a place
Before his eyes appeared, sad, noisome, dark,
A lazar-house it seemed, wherein were laid
Numbers of all diseased, all maladies,
Of ghastly spasm, or racking torture, qualms
Of heart-sick agony, all feverous kinds,

Convulsions, epilepsies, fierce catarrhs,
Intestine stone and ulcer, colic pangs,
Demoniac frenzy, moping melancholy,
And moon-struck madness, pining atrophy,
Marasmus, and wide-wasting pestilence,
Dropsies, and asthmas, and joint-racking rheums.

John Milton

DEATH THE LEVELLER

The glories of our blood and state
  Are shadows, not substantial things;
There is no armour against fate;
  Death lays his icy hand on kings:
    Sceptre and crown
    Must tumble down,
And in the dust be equal made
With the poor crooked scythe and spade.

James Shirley

DEATH SUMMONS EVERYMAN
from 'Everyman'

GOD   Where art thou, Death, thou mighty
             messenger?

DEATH   Almighty God, I am here at your will,
             Your commandment to fulfil.

GOD   Go thou to Everyman,
             And show him in my name
             A pilgrimage he must on him take,
             Which he in no wise may escape;

And that he bring with him a sure reckoning
Without delay or any tarrying.

DEATH   Lord, I will in the world go run over all
And cruelly outsearch both great and
    small. . . .
Lo, yonder I see Everyman walking;
Full little he thinketh on my coming. . . .
Everyman, stand still; whither art thou going
Thus gaily? Hast thou thy Maker forgot?

EVERYMAN   Why askst thou? Wouldest thou know?

DEATH   Yea, sir, I will show you;
In great haste I am sent to thee
From God out of his majesty.

EVERYMAN   What, sent to me?

DEATH   Yea, certainly.
Though thou have forget him here,
He thinketh on thee in the heavenly sphere,
As, or we depart, thou shalt know.

EVERYMAN   What desireth God of me?

DEATH   That shall I show thee;
A reckoning he will needs have
Without any longer respite. . . .

EVERYMAN   Full unready I am such reckoning to give.
I know thee not: what messenger art thou?

DEATH	I am Death, that no man dreadeth.
	For every man I rest and no man spareth;
	For it is God's commandment
	That all to me should be obedient.

EVERYMAN	O Death, thou camest when I had thee least in mind;
	In thy power it lieth me to save,
	Yet of my good will I give thee, if ye will be kind,
	Yea, a thousand pound shalt thou have,
	And defer this matter to another day.

DEATH	Everyman, it may not be by no way;
	I set not by gold, silver, nor riches,
	Nor by pope, emperor, king, duke, nor princes. . . .
	I give thee no respite: come hence, and not tarry.

EVERYMAN	Alas, shall I have no longer respite?
	I may say Death giveth no warning!
	To think on thee, it maketh my heart sick,
	For all unready is my book of reckoning. . . .

| DEATH | Thee availeth not to cry, weep, and pray. . . . |

EVERYMAN	Death, if I should this pilgrimage take,
	And my reckoning surely make,
	Show me, for saint charity,
	Should I not come again shortly?

DEATH	No, Everyman; and thou be once there,
	Thou mayst never more come here,
	Trust me verily.

EVERYMAN   O gracious God, in the high seat celestial,
            Have mercy on me in this most need;
            Shall I have no company from this vale
                terrestrial
            Of mine acquaintance that way me to lead?

DEATH   Yea, if any be so hardy,
            That would go with thee and bear thee
                company. . . .

EVERYMAN   O wretched caitiff, whither shall I flee,
            That I might scape this endless sorrow!
            Now, gentle Death, spare me till tomorrow,
            That I may amend me
            With good advisement.

DEATH   Nay, thereto I will not consent,
            Nor no man will I respite,
            But to the heart suddenly I shall smite
            Without any advisement.
            And now out of thy sight I will me hie;
            See thou make thee ready shortly,
            For thou mayst say this is the day
            That no man living may scape away.

                                        Anonymous

LONESOME VALLEY

When you walk that lonesome valley,
   You got to walk it by yourself.
No one here may walk it with you,
   You got to walk it by yourself.

When you reach the river Jordan,
   You got to cross it by yourself.
No one here may cross it with you,
   You got to cross it by yourself.

When you face that judgment morning,
   You got to face it by yourself.
No one here to face it for you,
   You got to face it by yourself.

Loud and strong your master calling,
   You got to answer by yourself.
No one here to answer for you,
   You got to answer by yourself.

Jordan's stream is cold and chilly,
   You got to stand it by yourself.
No one here to stand it for you,
   You got to stand it by yourself.

You got to stand your trial in judgment,
   You got to stand it by yourself.
No one here to stand it for you,
   You got to stand it by yourself.

                              Anonymous. Spiritual

OUT OF PARADISE
from 'Paradise Lost', Book XII

To their fixed station, all in bright array
The cherubim descended; on the ground
Gliding meteorous, as evening mist
Risen from a river o'er the marish glides,
And gathers ground fast at the labourer's heel
Homeward returning. High in front advanced
The brandished sword of God before them blazed,
Fierce as a comet; which with torrid heat,
And vapour as the Libyan air adust,
Began to parch that temperate clime; whereat
In either hand the hastening angel caught
Our lingering parents, and to the eastern gate
Led them direct, and down the cliff as fast
To the subjected plain; then disappeared.
They looking back, all the eastern side beheld
Of Paradise, so late their happy seat,
Waved over by that flaming brand, the gate
With dreadful faces thronged and fiery arms;
Some natural tears they dropped, but wiped them soon;
The world was all before them, where to choose
Their place of rest, and Providence their guide.
They hand in hand with wandering steps and slow
Through Eden took their solitary way.

John Milton

THE JUNK MAN

I am glad God saw Death
And gave Death a job taking care of all who are tired of
    living:

When all the wheels in a clock are worn and slow and the
    connections loose
And the clock goes on ticking and telling the wrong time
    from hour to hour
And people around the house joke about what a bum clock
    it is,
How glad the clock is when the big Junk Man drives his
    wagon
Up to the house and puts his arms around the clock and
    says :
        'You don't belong here,
        You gotta come
        Along with me,'
How glad the clock is then, when it feels the arms of the
Junk Man close around it and carry it away.

Carl Sandburg

DEAR BEAUTEOUS DEATH

Dear, beauteous death! the jewel of the just,
    Shining nowhere, but in the dark;
What mysteries do lie beyond thy dust;
    Could man outlook that mark!

He that hath found some fledged bird's nest, may know
    At first sight, if the bird be flown;
But what fair well, or grove he sings in now,
    That is to him unknown.

Henry Vaughan

III

Four thousand winters

ADAM LAY YBOUNDEN

Adam lay ybounden,
    Bounden in a bond,
Four thousand winters
    Thought he not too long.

And all was for an apple,
    An apple that he took,
As clerks finden written
    In their book.

Ne had the apple taken been,
    The apple taken been,
Ne had never our lady
    A-been heaven's queen.

Blessed be the time
    That apple taken was,
Therefore we moun singen
    Deo Gratias!

Anonymous

DE PROFUNDIS
from the Authorised Version of the Bible

Out of the depths have I cried unto thee, O Lord.

Lord, hear my voice: let thine ears be attentive to the voice of my supplications.

If thou, Lord, shouldest mark iniquities, O Lord, who shall stand?

But there is forgiveness with thee, that thou mayest be feared.

I wait for the Lord, my soul doth wait, and in his word do
   I hope.
My soul waiteth for the Lord more than they that watch
   for the morning : I say, more than they that watch for
   the morning.
Let Israel hope in the Lord : for with the Lord there is
   mercy, and with him is plenteous redemption.
And he shall redeem Israel from all his iniquities.

Psalm 130

ABRAHAM AND ISAAC
from 'The Chester Cycle'

GOD   Abraham, my servant Abraham!

ABRAHAM Lo, Lord already here I am.

GOD   Take Isaac, thy son by name
     That thou lovest best of all
     And in sacrifice offer him to me
     Upon that hill beside thee.
     Abraham, I will that it be so
     For aught that may befall.

ABRAHAM My Lord, to thee is my intent
     Always to be obedient;
     That son that thou hast sent
     Offer I will to thee. . . .

     Make thee ready, my Darling
     For we must do a little thing.
     This wood upon thy back thou bring,
     We must not long abide.

40

A sword and fire I will take,
For sacrifice I must make;
God's bidding I will not forsake
But ever obedient be.

ISAAC   Father, I am all ready
To do your bidding meekly.
To bear the wood full set am I
As you command me.

ABRAHAM   O Isaac, Isaac, my darling dear,
My blessing now I give thee here.
Take up this faggot with good cheer
And on thy back it bring.
Here the fire with me I take.

ISAAC   Your bidding I will not forsake,
Father, I will never be slack
To fulfil your bidding. . . .

ABRAHAM   O, my heart will break in three!
To hear thy words I have pity.
As thou wilt, Lord, so must it be
For thee I will obey.

Lay down thy faggot, my own dear son.

ISAAC   All ready, father, look it is here.
But why make you such heavy cheer?
Does anything make you dread?

Father now, if it be your will,
Where is the beast that we shall kill?

41

ABRAHAM   There is none, son, upon this hill
That I can see to strike dead.

ISAAC   Father, I am full sore afraid
To see your sword thus arrayed.
I hope, by all that is made,
You will not slay your child.

ABRAHAM   My child, I bid thee not dread:
Our Lord will send of his Godhead
Some kind of beast here instead,
Be it tame or wild.

ISAAC   Father, tell me ere I go
Whether I shall be harmed here or no.

ABRAHAM   Ah, dear God, this is such woe
As will burst my heart insunder.

ISAAC   Father, tell me what is amiss,
Why your sword is drawn out like this.
This naked blade frightens me, I wis,
And I am filled with deep wonder.

ABRAHAM   Isaac, son, peace! I pray thee,
Thou breakest my heart quite in three.

ISAAC   I pray you keep nothing from me
But tell me what you think.

ABRAHAM   O Isaac, Isaac, I must thee kill.

ISAAC   Alas, father, is that your will,
Your own child's life here to spill
Upon this hill's brink? . . .

ABRAHAM   O comely creature, unless I thee kill
I offend my God and that sore and ill.
I may not work against his high will
But ever obedient be. . . .

ISAAC   Father, since you needs must do so,
Let it pass quickly as it go;
Kneeling here before you low
Your blessing on me spread.

ABRAHAM   My blessing, dear son, give I thee
And thy mother's with heart so free.
The blessing of the Trinity,
My dear son, light on thee.

ISAAC   I pray you, father, cover my eyen,
That I see not your sword so keen;
That stroke must not be seen.
Say no more now to me. . . .

ANGEL   Abraham, my servant dear.

ABRAHAM   Lo, lord, I am already here.

ANGEL   Lay not thy sword in no manner
On Isaac, thy dear darling.

Nay! do him no injury.
For thou dreadest God, well I see
That on thy son thou hast no mercy
To do his bidding. . . .

ABRAHAM   Ah, Lord of heaven and King of bliss,
Thy bidding I shall do in this.

Sacrifice here to me sent is
And all, Lord, through thy grace.

A horned wether here I see
Among the briars tied is he.
Offered to thee it shall be
Anon right in this place.

GOD   Abraham, by my self I swear
Thou hast been so obedient e'er
And spared not thy son so dear
To fulfil my bidding.

Thou shall be blessed, thou art worthy
Thy seed I shall multiply
As the stars and sand, so say I,
Of thy body coming.

And all nations, believe thou me,
Blessed ever more shall be
Through fruit that shall come of thee
And all the good be made glad.

Anonymous, translated by Maurice Hussey

INTERCESSION AGAINST THE PLAGUE

Set free thy people, set free thy servants,
Lighten thine anger, Ruler most holy;
Look on their anguish, bitter their weeping,
                    Christ, in thy mercy.

Thou art our Father, Master exalted,
We are thy servants, thou the Good Shepherd,
Bearing thy token of blood and of crimson
                    Marked on our foreheads.

Deep in thy hell who then shall confess thee?
Yea, shall the dead give praise to thy name?
Judge of our dread, thy rod is of iron,
>   Spare us, we pray thee.

Bring not so near to thy people, thy servants,
The cup of thine anger, thy merited wrath:
Lighten upon us thine ancient compassion.
>   We cry. Do thou hear!

Loosen, we pray thee, our load of transgression.
Vouchsafe to keep us, Prince ever blessed.
Vanquish the shadow that darkens our spirits,
>   Light of the world.

Saint of all saints and king of all kingships,
Visit thy people with thy right hand.
Lift up the light of thy countenance upon us,
>   Lord, or we perish.

>   *Sedulius Scottus*, translated by Helen Waddell

GO DOWN MOSES

>   Go down Moses,
>   Way down in Egypt land,
>   Tell old Pharaoh
>   To let my people go.

When Israel was in Egypt land
>   (*Let my people go*)
Oppressed so hard they could not stand.
>   (*Let my people go*)

'Thus spake the Lord,' bold Moses said,
    '*Let my people go,*
If not, I'll strike your firstborn dead.
    Let my people go.'

        Go down, Moses,
        Way down in Egypt land,
        Tell old Pharaoh
        To let my people go.

                Anonymous. Spiritual

LEAD, KINDLY LIGHT

Lead, kindly light, amid th' encircling gloom,
    Lead thou me on!
The night is dark, and I am far from home,
    Lead thou me on!
Keep thou my feet; I do not ask to see
The distant scene — one step enough for me.

I was not ever thus, nor prayed that thou
    Shouldst lead me on.
I loved to see and choose my path, but now
    Lead thou me on!
I loved the garish day, and, spite of fears,
Pride ruled my will; remember not past years.

So long thy power hath blest me, sure it still
    Will lead me on,
O'er moor and fen, o'er crag and torrent, till
    The night is gone;
And with the morn those angel faces smile,
Which I have loved long since, and lost awhile.

                John Henry Newman

SAMSON AGONISTES
from 'Samson Agonistes'

O dark, dark, dark amid the blaze of noon,
Irrecoverably dark, total eclipse
Without all hope of day!
O first created beam, and thou great word,
'Let there be light,' and light was over all,
Why am I thus bereaved thy prime decree?
The sun to me is dark
And silent as the moon,
When she deserts the night
Hid in her vacant interlunar cave.
Since life so necessary is to life,
And almost life itself, if it be true
That light is in the soul,
She all in every part; why was the sight
To such a tender ball as th' eye confined?
So obvious and so easy to be quenched,
And not as feeling through all parts diffused,
That she might look at will through every pore?
Then had I not been thus exiled from light;
As in the land of darkness yet in light,
To live a life half dead, a living death,
And buried; but O yet more miserable!
My self, my sepulchre, a moving grave,
Buried, yet not exempt
By privilege of death and burial
From worst of other evils, pains and wrongs,
But made hereby obnoxious more
To all the miseries of life,
Life in captivity
Among inhuman foes.

John Milton

ALL BUT BLIND

All but blind
   In his chambered hole
Gropes for worms
   The four-clawed Mole.

All but blind
   In the evening sky
The hooded Bat
   Twirls softly by.

All but blind
   In the burning day
The Barn-Owl blunders
   On her way.

And blind as are
   These three to me,
So, blind to Some-One
   I must be.

Walter de la Mare

POOR WAYFARING STRANGER

I am a poor wayfaring stranger
   While travelling through this world of woe,
Yet there's no sickness, toil nor danger
   In that bright world to which I go.
I'm going there to see my father,
   I'm going there no more to roam,
I'm only going over Jordan,
   I'm only going over home.

I know dark clouds will gather round me,
    I know my way is rough and steep;
Yet beauteous fields lie just before me
    Where God's redeemed their vigils keep.
I'm going there to see my mother,
    She said she'd meet me when I come,
I'm only going over Jordan,
    I'm only going over home.

Anonymous. Spiritual

DANIEL

Darius the Mede was a king and a wonder.
His eye was proud, and his voice was thunder.
He kept bad lions in a monstrous den.
He fed up the lions on Christian men.

Daniel was the chief hired man of the land.
He stirred up the music in the palace band.
He whitewashed the cellar. He shovelled in the coal.
And Daniel kept a-praying :— 'Lord save my soul.'
Daniel kept a-praying :— 'Lord save my soul.'
Daniel kept a-praying :— 'Lord save my soul.'

Daniel was the butler, swagger and swell.
He ran up stairs. He answered the bell.
And *he* would let in whoever came a-calling :—
Saints so holy, scamps so appalling.
'Old man Ahab leaves his card.
Elisha and the bears are a-waiting in the yard.
Here comes Pharaoh and his snakes a-calling.
Here comes Cain and his wife a-calling.
Shadrach, Meshach and Abednego for tea.
Here comes Jonah and the whale,

And the *Sea*!
Here comes St. Peter and his fishing pole.
Here comes Judas and his silver a-calling.
Here comes old Beelzebub a-calling.'
And Daniel kept a-praying :— 'Lord save my soul.'
And Daniel kept a-praying :— 'Lord save my soul.'
Daniel kept a-praying :— 'Lord save my soul.'

His sweetheart and his mother were Christian and meek.
They washed and ironed for Darius every week.
One Thursday he met them at the door :—
Paid them as usual, but acted sore.

He said :— 'Your Daniel is a dead little pigeon.
He's a good hard worker, but he talks religion.'
And he showed them Daniel in the lions' cage.
Daniel standing quietly, the lions in a rage.

His good old mother cried :—
'Lord save him.'
And Daniel's tender sweetheart cried :—
'Lord save him!'

And she was a golden lily in the dew.
And she was as sweet as an apple on the tree
And she was as fine as a melon in the cornfield,
Gliding and lovely as a ship on the sea,
Gliding and lovely as a ship on the sea.

And she prayed to the Lord :—
'Send Gabriel! Send Gabriel!'

King Darius said to the lions :—
'Bite Daniel. Bite Daniel.
Bite him. Bite him. Bite him.'

Thus roared the lions :—
'We want Daniel, Daniel, Daniel,
We want Daniel, Daniel, Daniel.'

And Daniel did not frown,
Daniel did not cry.
He kept on looking at the sky.
And the Lord said to Gabriel :—
'Go chain the lions down,
Go chain the lions down,
Go chain the lions down,
Go chain the lions down.'

And *Gabriel* chained the lions,
And *Gabriel* chained the lions,
And *Gabriel* chained the lions,
And Daniel got out of the den,
And Daniel got out of the den,
And Daniel got out of the den,
And Darius said :— 'You're a Christian child,'
Darius said :— 'You're a Christian child,'
Darius said :— 'You're a Christian child,'
And gave him his job again,
And gave him his job again,
And gave him his job again.

Vachel Lindsay

JUSTORUM ANIMAE
from the Authorised Version of the Bible

But the souls of the righteous are in the hand of God, and
there shall no torment touch them.
In the sight of the unwise they seemed to die : and their
departure is taken for misery.

And their going from us to be utter destruction; but they
are in peace.

For though they be punished in the sight of man, yet is
their hope full of immortality.

And having been a little chastened, they shall be greatly
rewarded : for God proved them, and found them
worthy of himself.

As gold in the furnace hath he tried them, and received
them as a burnt offering.

And in the time of their visitation they shall shine, and run
to and fro like sparks among the stubble.

They shall judge nations, and have dominion over the
people, and their Lord shall reign for ever.

They that put their trust in him shall understand the truth,
and such as be faithful in love shall abide with
him : for grace and mercy is to his saints, and he
hath care for his elect.

The Book of Wisdom, Chapter III

THE PULLEY

When God at first made man,
Having a glass of blessings standing by,
Let us, said he, pour on him all we can;
Let the world's riches, which dispersed lie,
Contract into a span.

So strength first made a way;
Then beauty flowed, then wisdom, honour, pleasure;
When almost all was out, God made a stay,
Perceiving that alone of all his treasure,
Rest in the bottom lay.

52

For if I should, said he,
Bestow this jewel also on my creature,
He would adore my gifts instead of me,
And rest in nature, not the God of nature :
    So both should losers be.

Yet let him keep the rest,
But keep them with repining restlessness,
Let him be rich and weary, that at least,
If goodness lead him not, yet weariness
    May toss him to my breast.

George Herbert

WARM BABIES

Shadrach, Meshach, Abednego,
Walked in the furnace to an' fro,
Hayfoot, strawfoot, fro an' to,
An' the flame an' the smoke flared up the flue.
Nebuchadnezzar he listen some,
An' he hear 'em talk, an' he say 'How come?'
An' he hear 'em walk, an' he say 'How so?
Dem babes was hawg-tied an hour ago!'
Then Shadrach call, in an uppity way :
'A little more heat, or we ain' gwine stay!'
An' Meshach bawl, so dat furnace shake;
'Lan'lawd, heat! fo' de good Lawd's sake!'
Abednego yell, with a loud 'Kerchoo!'
'Is you out to freeze us, y' great big Jew!'

Nebuchadnezzar, he rare an' ramp,
An' call to the janitor, 'You big black scamp!
Shake dem clinkers an' spend dat coal!
I'll bake dem birds, ef I goes in de hole!'

53

So he puts on de draf an' he shuts de door
So de furnace glow an' de chimbly roar.
Ol' Nebuchadnezzar he smole a smile.
'Guess dat'll hold 'em,' says he, 'one while.'

Then Shadrach, Meshach, Abednego,
Walk on de hot coals to an' fro,
Gulp dem cinders like chicken meat,
An' holler out for a mite mo' heat.
Ol' Nebuchadnezzar gives up de fight;
He opens dat door, an' he bows perlite.
He shade his eyes from the glare infernal
An' say to Abednego, 'Step out, Colonel.'
An' he add, 'Massa Shadrach, I hopes you all
Won' be huffy at me at all.'

Then Shadrach, Meshach, Abednego,
Hayfoot, strawfoot, three in a row,
Stepped right smart from the oven door,
Jes' as good as they wuz before,
An', far as Nebuchadnezzar could find,
Jes' as good as they wuz behind.

Keith Preston

ON THE NEEDLE OF A SUNDIAL

Behold this needle : when the Arctick stone
Has touched it, how it trembles up and down;
Hunts for the Pole; and cannot be possessed
Of peace, until it find that point, that rest.
Such is the heart of man : which, when it hath
Attained the virtue of a lively faith,
It finds no rest on earth, makes no abode
In any object, but his heaven, his God.

Francis Quarles

54

IV

Comfort ye
my people

IV

Comfort ye
my people

MESSIAH

from the Authorised Version of the Bible

The people that walked in darkness
    have seen a great light :
they that dwell in the land of the shadow of death,
    upon them hath the light shined. . . .
For unto us a child is born,
    unto us a son is given;
and the government shall be upon his shoulder :
    and his name shall be called
Wonderful, Counsellor, the Mighty God,
    the Everlasting Father, the Prince of Peace.
Of the increase of his government and peace
    there shall be no end,
upon the throne of David, and upon his kingdom,
    to order it, and to establish it,
with judgment and with justice
    from henceforth even for ever.

Isaiah, Chapter IX

HARK A THRILLING VOICE IS SOUNDING

Hark! a thrilling voice is sounding;
'Christ is nigh,' it seems to say;
'Cast away your dreams of darkness,
O ye children of the day!'

Wakened by the solemn warning,
Let the earth-bound soul arise;
Christ her sun, all ill dispelling,
Shines upon the morning skies.

Edward Caswall

THE EXPECTATION

Over the apple trees with their red load
In world's end orchards, over dark yew woods,
O'er fires of sunset glassed in wizard streams,
O'er milk and meadow of those farthest lands,
Over the reapers, over the sere sails
Of homing ships and every breaking wave,
Over the haven and the entranced town,
O'er hearths aflame with fir-trunks and fir-cones,
Over the children playing in the streets,
Over the harpers harping on the bridge,
O'er lovers in their dream and their desire,
There falls from the high heaven a subtle sense
Of presage and a deep expectant hush,
And the wise watchers know the time draws on
And that amid the snows of that same year
The earth will bear her perfect, longed-for fruit.

R. L. Gales

MARY AND GABRIEL
from 'The Wakefield Cycle'

GABRIEL   Hail Mary gracious!
Hail, maiden and God's spouse!
   To thee I bow devout,
Of all virgins thou art queen
That ever was or shall be seen,
   Without a doubt. . . .

For thou hast found, without a doubt,
The grace of God that has gone out
   For Adam's plight.

58

This is the grace that gives thee bloom,
Thou shalt conceive within thy womb
   A child of might.

When he is come, that is thy son,
He shall take circumcision,
   Call him Jesus.
God's son men shall him call,
Who comes to free the thrall
   Within us.

MARY   What is thy name?

GABRIEL   Gabriel,
God's strength and his angel,
   That comes to thee.

MARY   Wondrous words are in thy greeting,
But to bear God's gentle sweeting,
   How should it be?

I slept never by man's side,
But in maidhood would abide
   Unshaken.
Therefore, I know not how
This may be, because a vow
   I have taken. . . .

GABRIEL   Lady, this the secret hear of me;
The holy ghost shall come to thee,
   And in this virtue
Thee enshroud and so infuse,
Yet thou thy maidhood shall not lose,
   But ay be new. . . .

MARY   My lord's love will I not withstand,
I am his maiden at his hand,
     And in his fold.
Gabriel, I believe that God will bring
To pass with me each several thing
     As thou hast told. . . .

JOSEPH   Almighty God, what may this be!
Mary, my wife, amazes me,
     Herself she has forgot.
Her body is great, she is with child!
By me she never was defiled,
     Mine therefore it is not. . . .

She is with child, I know not how;
Who could trust any woman now?
     No man of any good;
I know not what now I should do,
Save go to her and ask her who
     Shall own the fatherhood.

Hail, Mary, and well ye be!
Why, but woman, what cheer with thee?

MARY   The better, sir, for you.

JOSEPH   So would I, woman, that ye were;
A mock now Mary you'll incur
     And your state sadly rue.

But one thing I must ask of thee,
The child's father, who is he?

MARY   Sir, ye, and God of heaven.

JOSEPH   Mine, Mary? Leave be thy din,
Ye know I have no part therein,
    Swear it, by those stars seven.

MARY   By God's will, Joseph, must it be,
For certainly save God and thee
    I know no other man;
Nor in flesh have been defiled.

JOSEPH   How then, art thou thus with child?
    Excuse that, if ye can. . . .

God's and mine she says it is;
I will not father it, she says amiss;
    With shame she is beset
To excuse her villainy to me.
With her I can no longer be,
    I rue that ever we met.

GABRIEL   Be warned, Joseph, and change thy thought,
Which to wandering thee has brought,
    In the wilderness so wild;
Turn home to thy spouse again,
Thy wife she is without a stain,
    Nor ever was defiled.

Tax not from heaven the heavenly host,
She has conceived the holy ghost,
    And God's son she shall bear.
Therefore with her, in thy degree,
Meek and obedient, look thou be
    And of her take good care. . . .

JOSEPH	Ah, Mary, wife, what cheer?
MARY	The better, sir, that ye are here; Thus long where have you been?
JOSEPH	Fretting and walking up and down, And troubled how to smooth thy frown Against my thoughts unclean. . . .
MARY	Now all that ever ye said to me, God forgives as I do thee, With all the might I may. . . .

JOSEPH	Lo, I am as light as a leaf!
	He that can quench all grief
	    And every wrong amend,
	Lend me grace, power and might,
	My wife and her sweet son of light
	    To keep to my life's end.

Anonymous, edited by Martial Rose

HER NATIVITY

For God in earth she is the royal throne,
  The chosen cloth to make his mortal weed;
The quarry to cut out our corner-stone,
  Soil full of, yet free from, all mortal seed;
For heavenly flower she is the Jesse rod,
The child of man, the parent of a God.

Robert Southwell

THE ANNUNCIATION

Nothing will ease the pain to come
Though now she sits in ecstasy
And lets it have its way with her.
The angel's shadow in the room
Is lightly lifted as if he
Had never terrified her there.

The furniture again returns
To its old simple state. She can
Take comfort from the things she knows
Though in her heart new loving burns,
Something she never gave to man
Or god before, and this god grows

Most like a man. She wonders how
To pray at all, what thanks to give
And whom to give them to. 'Alone
To all men's eyes I now must go'
She thinks, 'And by myself must live
With a strange child that is my own.'

So from her ecstasy she moves
And turns to human things at last
(Announcing angels set aside).
It is a human child she loves
Though a god stirs beneath her breast
And great salvations grip her side.

Elizabeth Jennings

63

MARY OF NAZARETH

It was like music :
Hovering and floating there
With the sound of lutes and timbrels
In the night air.

It was like waves,
Beating upon the shore :
Insistent with a rhythm, a pulsing
Unfelt before.

It was like wind :
Blowing from off the seas
Of other, far other
Lands than these.

It was like wings,
Like whirring wings that fly —
The song of an army of swans
On the dark sky.

It was like God :
A presence of blinding light,
Ravishing body and soul
In the Spring night.

Clive Sansom

THE CHERRY TREE CAROL

As Joseph and Mary were a-walking the green,
They was apples and cherries plenty there to be seen.

And then Mary said to Joseph, so meek and so mild :
Gather me some cherries, Joseph, for I am with child.

Then Joseph said to Mary so rough and unkind :
Let the daddy of the baby get the cherries for thine.

Then the baby spoke out of its mother's womb :
Bow down you lofty cherry trees, let my mammy have
     some.

Then the cherry tree bent and it bowed like a bow,
So that Mary picked cherries from the uppermost bough.

Then Joseph took Mary all on his left knee,
Saying : Lord have mercy on me and what I have done.

Then Joseph took Mary all on his right knee,
Saying : O my little Saviour, when your birthday shall be,
The hills and high mountains shall bow unto thee.

Then the baby spoke out of its mother's womb :
On old Christmas morning my birthday shall be,
When the hills and high mountains shall bow unto me.

Anonymous. Appalachian Folk Song

COMFORT YE MY PEOPLE
from the Authorised Version of the Bible

Comfort ye, comfort ye my people,
    saith your God.
Speak ye comfortably to Jerusalem,
    and cry unto her
that her warfare is accomplished,
    that her iniquity is pardoned :
for she has received of the Lord's hand
    double for all her sins.

The voice of him that crieth in the wilderness,
  'Prepare ye the way of the Lord,
  make straight in the desert a highway for our God.'
Every valley shall be exalted,
  and every mountain and hill shall be made low;
and the crooked shall be made straight
  and the rough places plain :
and the glory of the Lord shall be revealed,
  and all flesh shall see it together :
  for the mouth of the Lord hath spoken it.

Isaiah, Chapter XL

ST. JOHN THE BAPTIST

The last and greatest herald of heaven's king,
Girt with rough skins, hies to the deserts wild,
Among that savage brood the woods forth bring
Which he than man more harmless found and mild :

His food was locusts, and what young doth spring,
With honey that from virgin hives distilled;
Parched body, hollow eyes, some uncouth thing
Made him appear long since from earth exiled.

There burst he forth : 'All ye, whose hopes rely
On God, with me amidst these deserts mourn;
Repent, repent, and from old errors turn.'
Who listened to his voice, obeyed his cry ?

  Only the echoes which he made relent,
  Rung from their marble caves, *Repent, repent*.

William Drummond

ST. JOHN BAPTIST

I, John, not reed but root;
Not vested priest nor saviour but a voice
Crying daylong like a cricket in the heat,
Demand your worship. Not of me
But of the traveller I am calling
From beyond Jordan and the limestone hills,
Whose runner and rude servant I am only.
Not man entirely but God's watchman,
I dwell among these blistered rocks
Awaiting the wide dawn, the wonder
Of His first coming, and the Dove's descent.

Sidney Keyes

HEY THE GIFT, HO THE GIFT

Hey the Gift, ho the Gift,
Hey the Gift, on the living.

> Son of the dawn, Son of the clouds,
> Son of the planet, Son of the star.

Hey the Gift, ho the Gift,
Hey the Gift, on the living.

> Son of the rain, Son of the dew,
> Son of the welkin, Son of the sky.

> Son of the flame, Son of the light,
> Son of the sphere, Son of the globe.

> Son of the elements, Son of the heavens,
> Son of the moon, Son of the sun.

Son of Mary of the God-mind,
And the Son of God first of all news.

Hey the Gift, ho the Gift,
Hey the Gift, on the living.
Anonymous. Gaelic, translated by Alexander Carmichael

IN THE TOWN

JOSEPH   Take heart, the journey's ended,
         I see the twinkling lights
       Where we shall be befriended
         On this the night of nights.

MARY   Now praise the Lord that led us
         So safe into the town,
       Where men will feed and bed us,
         And I can lay me down.

JOSEPH   And how then shall we praise him?
         Alas, my heart is sore
       That we no gifts can raise him,
         We are so very poor.

MARY   We have as much as any
         That on the earth do live,
       Although we have no penny,
         We have ourselves to give.

JOSEPH   Look yonder, wife, look yonder!
         A hostelry I see,
       Where travellers that wander
         Will very welcome be.

MARY   The house is tall and stately,
            The door stands open thus;
        Yet, husband, I fear greatly
            That inn is not for us.

JOSEPH God save you, gentle master!
            Your littlest room indeed
        With plainest walls of plaster
            Tonight will serve our need.

HOST   For lordlings and for ladies
            I've lodging and to spare;
        For you and yonder maid is
            No closet anywhere.

JOSEPH Take heart, take heart, sweet Mary,
            Another inn I spy,
        Whose host will not be chary
            To let us easy lie.

MARY   O aid me, I am ailing,
            My strength is nearly gone;
        I feel my limbs are failing,
            And yet we must go on.

JOSEPH God save you, hostess, kindly!
            I pray you, house my wife,
        Who bears beside me blindly
            The burden of her life.

HOSTESS My guests are rich men's daughters
            And sons, I'd have you know!
        Seek out the poorer quarters
            Where ragged people go.

JOSEPH	Good sir, my wife's in labour, Some corner let us keep.
HOST	Not I; knock up my neighbour, And as for me, I'll sleep.

MARY	In all the lighted city
	    Where rich men welcome win,
	Will not one house for pity
	    Take two poor strangers in?

JOSEPH	Good woman, I implore you, Afford my wife a bed.
HOSTESS	Nay, nay, I've nothing for you, Except the cattle shed.

MARY	Then gladly in the manger
	    Our bodies we will house,
	Since men tonight are stranger
	    Than asses are and cows.

JOSEPH	Take heart, take heart, sweet Mary,
	    The cattle are our friends,
	Lie down, lie down, sweet Mary,
	    For here our journey ends.

MARY	Now praise the Lord that found me
	    This shelter in the town,
	Where I with friends around me
	    May lay my burden down.

Anonymous

70

NIGHT OF MARVELS

I saw the trembling fire look wan,
I saw the sun shed tears of blood,
I saw a God become a man,
I saw a man become a God.

Sister Violante do Ceo, translated by John Bowring

IF YE WOULD HEAR THE ANGELS SING

If ye would hear the angels sing
'Peace on earth and mercy mild,'
Think of him who was once a child
On Christmas Day in the morning.

If ye would hear the angels sing,
Christians! see ye let each door
Stand wider than ever it stood before,
On Christmas Day in the morning.

Rise, and open wide the door;
Christians, rise! the world is wide,
And many there be that stand outside,
Yet Christmas comes in the morning.

If ye would hear the angels sing,
Rise, and spread your Christmas fare;
'Tis merrier still the more that share
On Christmas Day in the morning.

Rise, and bake your Christmas bread;
Christians, rise! the world is bare,
And blank, and dark with want and care,
Yet Christmas comes in the morning.

If ye would hear the angels sing,
Rise, and light your Christmas fire;
And see that ye pile the logs still higher
On Christmas Day in the morning.

Rise, and light your Christmas fire;
Christians, rise! the world is old,
And Time is weary, and worn, and cold,
Yet Christmas comes in the morning.

If ye would hear the angels sing,
Rise and spice your wassail bowl
With warmth for body, and heart, and soul,
On Christmas Day in the morning.

Spice it warm, and spice it strong,
Christians, rise! the world is grey,
And rough is the road, and short is the day,
Yet Christmas comes in the morning.

Dora Greenwell

Christmas Eve
and twelve
of the clock

V

Christmas Eve
and twelve
of the clock

OF A ROSE, A LOVELY ROSE,
OF A ROSE IS ALL MY SONG

Listen, lordings, both old and young,
How this rose began to spring,
Such a rose to my liking,
  In all this world know I none.

The angel came from heaven's tower,
To greet Mary with great honour,
And said she should bear the flower
  That should break the fiend's bond.

The flower sprang in high Bethlehem,
That is both bright and sheen;
The rose is Mary, heaven's queen,
  Out of her the blossom sprung.

The first branch is full of might,
That sprang on Christmas night,
The star shone over Bethlehem bright
  That is both broad and long.

The second branch sprang down to hell,
The fiend's power down to fell;
Therein no soul might dwell —
  Blessed be the time the rose sprung!

The third branch is good and sweet,
It sprang to heaven, crop and root,
There to dwell and do us good,
  Every day it shows in the priest's hand.

Pray me to her with great honour,
She that bore the blessed flower,

May she be our help and our succour,
And shield us from the fiend's bond.

Anonymous

HAIL JOHN'S ARMY

Hail John's army, bend down and die,
Hail John's army, bend down and die.

Clock up in heaven done struck one :
(*Bend down and die*)
The good Lord Jesus was Mary's son.
(*Bend down and die*)

Clock up in heaven done struck two :
Jesus Christ was born a Jew.

Clock up in heaven done struck three :
Jesus Christ can make a blind man see.

Clock up in heaven done struck four :
Jesus Christ can make a rich man poor.

Clock up in heaven done struck five :
Jesus Christ can make a dead man alive.

Clock up in heaven done struck six :
Jesus Christ can help you in a fix.

Clock up in heaven done struck seven :
Jesus Christ got the key of heaven.

Clock up in heaven done struck eight :
Jesus got the key to the pearly gate.

76

Clock up in heaven done struck nine :
Jesus Christ turned water to wine.

Clock up in heaven done struck ten :
Jesus died on the cross to save all men.

Clock up in heaven done struck eleven :
Jesus Christ shows sinners the way to heaven.

Hail, John's army, bend down and die,
Hail, John's army, bend down and die.

Clock up in heaven done struck twelve :
           (*Bend down and die*)
Jesus Christ says do all things well.
           (*Bend down and die*).

           Anonymous. Spiritual

CHANTICLEER

All this night shrill chanticleer,
Day's proclaiming trumpeter,
   Claps his wings and loudly cries :
   Mortals, mortals, wake and rise !
      See a wonder,
      Heaven is under :
From the earth is risen a sun
Shines all night, though day be done.

Wake, O earth, wake everything !
Wake and hear the joy I bring ;
   Wake and joy ; for all this night
   Heaven and every twinkling light,

All amazing,
Still stand gazing.
Angels, Powers, and all that be,
Wake, and joy this sun to see!

Hail, O sun, O blessed light!
Sent into the world by night!
Let thy rays and heavenly powers
Shine in these dark souls of ours;
For most duly
Thou art truly
God and man, we do confess:
Hail, O Sun of Righteousness!

William Austin

ST. JOSEPH AND GOD'S MOTHER

St. Joseph and God's Mother,
They kept good company,
And they rode out of Nazareth
So early in the day.

They found no place to rest in,
No place in all the town,
And there they made an arbour,
Of reeds and grasses brown.

St. Joseph went to look for fire,
No fire there could he see,
And when he came to Mary,
The Babe was on her knee,
As white as is the milk,
As red as rose was He.

St. Joseph looked upon Him:
    'O what is this fair thing?
This is no child of mine,
    This comes from heaven's King.'

By there came three shepherds
    To wish Him a good day,
The two upon their fiddles,
    The third his bells did play.

And there they played sweet music,
    All for to make Him mirth;
Three hours have not gone yet
    Since our Saviour's birth.

'Dance, Maiden Mary,
    Dance, Mother mild,
And if you will dance with me,
    The ass will hold the Child.'

'I will not dance, Joseph,
    My husband so dear,
But if you will dance for joy,
    Dance, husband, here.'

Joseph then began to dance
    With all his might and main;
The mother smiled and said to him
    'Joseph is young again.'

'And if I rejoice, Mary,
    Well ought that to be;
Here is born to us tonight
    The King of glory.'

Anonymous. Spanish ballad, translated by Edith C. Batho

THE STABLE

I saw a stable low and very bare,
  A little child in a manger.
The oxen knew him, had him in their care,
  To men he was a stranger.
The safety of the world was lying there,
  And the world's danger.

Mary Coleridge

ADORATION OF THE SHEPHERDS
from 'The Chester Cycle'

FIRST SHEPHERD

> Ho! Hullo, there, ho, ho!
> Drive all the sheep down low.
> They may not hear unless I do blow;
>   Now out my horn shall bay.

SECOND SHEPHERD

> Hullo, now be well met!
> One thing only we need is
> That Tod should here be set
>   Then we might sit and feed us.

FIRST SHEPHERD

> Call him 'Tod, Tib's son',
> Ay, then he will come,
> For he will always run
>   At his mother's name.

SECOND SHEPHERD

> Now Tod! Tib's son!

THIRD SHEPHERD

>Sir, see, here I come
>Though I have not all done
>>What I have begun. . . .

SECOND SHEPHERD

>Now, since God has gathered us together
>With good heart I thank Him for His grace.
>Welcome are you as is fair weather :
>Tod, shall we all take some solace ?

THIRD SHEPHERD

>Ay, here is bread this day was made,
>Onions, garlic and leeks,
>Butter and eggs this day were laid
>And green cheese to grease your cheeks.

>And here ale of Halton I have
>And what meat I had for my hire;
>A pudding may no man deprave,
>And an oat-cake from Lancashire.

>Look, here's a sheep's head soused in ale,
>And a loin to lay on the green,
>And sour milk my wife had on sale
>A noble supper as may be seen.

FIRST SHEPHERD

>And as it is seen, ye shall see
>What things I have here in my sack :
>A pig's foot I have here, pardee !
>A dish of cold tripe in my pack.

A sausage, fellows, now have I,
A liver too I do not lack;
Chittrelings boiled this must be.
Such burden I bear on my back. . . .

SECOND SHEPHERD

Housing enough have we here
While we have Heaven over our heads;
Now to wet our mouths time it were.
This flagon I broach, no more said.

FIRST SHEPHERD

What is all this light here
That shines so bright here
    On my black beard?
For to see this sight here
A man may take fright here
    For I am afraid. . . .

THIRD SHEPHERD

Such a sight seeming,
And a light gleaming,
    I am afraid to look.
All this bright beaming
From a star streaming.
    I am sore struck.

ANGEL

Gloria in excelsis Deo,
Et in terra pax
Hominibus bonae voluntatis.

Shepherds, of this sight
Be ye not afright
For this is God's might,
  Take this in mind!

To Bethlehem go now right
There you shall see in sight
That Christ is born tonight
  To redeem all mankind.

FIRST SHEPHERD

To Bethlehem take the way.
Over the hills let us wend
That prince of peace to pray
Heaven to have at our end.

THIRD SHEPHERD

Sim! Sim! Securely
Here I see Mary
And Jesu Christ fast by,
  Lapped in the hay.

SECOND SHEPHERD

Kneel we down all three
And pray we him for mercy;
And welcome him worthily
  That drives woe away. . . .

FIRST SHEPHERD

Come we near anon
With such as we have brought,
Ring, brush or precious stone;
  Let's see whether we have aught. . . .

Lo! I bring thee a bell;
I pray thee, save me from hell
That I may with thee dwell
    And fare well for aye.

SECOND SHEPHERD

I bring thee a flask and a spoon
To eat thy pottage withal at noon
As I myself so oft have done.
    With heart, I pray thee, take it.

THIRD SHEPHERD

The gift I bring thee is but small,
Though I come up last of all.
I bring but a cap to thy stall,
    But Lord, think still on me.

FIRST SHEPHERD

Now farewell, mother and may,
For of sin naught thou knowest,
Thou hast brought forth this day
God's son which in might is the most.

SECOND SHEPHERD

Brethren, let us all three,
Singing, walk homewards.
Unkind will I never be
But preach what I can and cry
As Gabriel taught by his grace to me,
Singing always hence will I.

THIRD SHEPHERD

Over the sea, and I may have grace,
I will pass and about go now

To preach this in every place;
And sheep will I keep no more now.

FIRST SHEPHERD

And I an hermit
Praise to God to pay,
To walk by sty and street,
In wilderness to walk for aye. . . .

THIRD SHEPHERD

To that bliss bring us,
Great God, if it thy will be
Amend all things that are amiss.
Good men, now farewell to ye.

FIRST SHEPHERD

Well to fare, too, dear friend,
God of his might grant to you;
For here now we make an end.
Farewell for we from you must go too.

Anonymous, translated by Maurice Hussey

BETHLEHEM

O little town of Bethlehem,
    How still we see thee lie!
Above thy deep and dreamless sleep
    The silent stars go by.
Yet in thy dark streets shineth
    The everlasting light —
The hopes and fears of all the years
    Are met in thee tonight.

Phillips Brooks

THE OXEN

Christmas Eve, and twelve of the clock.
'Now they are all on their knees,'
An elder said as we sat in a flock
By the embers in hearthside ease.

We pictured the meek mild creatures where
They dwelt in their strawy pen,
Nor did it occur to one of us there
To doubt they were kneeling then.

So fair a fancy few would weave
In these years! Yet, I feel,
If someone said on Christmas Eve,
'Come; see the oxen kneel

In the lonely barton by yonder coomb
Our childhood used to know,'
I should go with him in the gloom,
Hoping it might be so.

Thomas Hardy

SANS DAY CAROL

Now the holly bears a berry as white as the milk,
And Mary bore Jesus, who was wrapped up in silk.

> *And Mary bore Jesus Christ our Saviour for to be,*
> *And the first tree in the greenwood it was the*
> *holly, holly, holly,*
> *And the first tree in the greenwood, it was the*
> *holly.*

Now the holly bears a berry as green as the grass,
And Mary bore Jesus, who died on the cross.

Now the holly bears a berry as black as the coal,
And Mary bore Jesus who died for us all.

Now the holly bears a berry, as blood it is red,
Then trust we our saviour, who rose from the dead.

> *And Mary bore Jesus Christ our Saviour for to be,*
> *And the first tree in the greenwood it was the*
> *holly, holly, holly,*
> *And the first tree in the greenwood, it was the*
> *holly.*

Anonymous

HARK HOW ALL THE WELKIN RINGS

Hark! how all the welkin rings
Glory to the king of kings.
Peace on earth, and mercy mild,
God and sinners reconciled.
Joyful, all ye nations rise,
Join the triumph of the skies;
With the angelic host proclaim :
'Christ is born in Bethlehem.'
> Hark! how all the welkin rings
> Glory to the king of kings.

Hail, the heaven-born prince of peace!
Hail, the sun of righteousness!
Light and life to all he brings,
Risen with healing in his wings.
Mild he lays his glory by,

Born that man no more may die,
Born to raise the sons of earth,
Born to give them second birth,
　　Hark! how all the welkin rings
　　Glory to the king of kings.

Charles Wesley

A CHRISTMAS CAROL

'The Chief Constable has issued a statement declaring that carol singing in the streets by children is illegal, and morally and physically injurious. He appeals to the public to discourage the practice.'
(Daily paper)

God rest you merry gentlemen,
Let nothing you dismay;
The Herald Angels cannot sing,
The cops arrest them on the wing,
And warn them of the docketing
Of anything they say.

God rest you merry gentlemen,
Let nothing you dismay:
On your reposeful cities lie
Deep silence, broken only by
The motor-horn's melodious cry,
The hooter's happy bray.

So, when the song of children ceased
And Herod was obeyed,
In his high hall Corinthian
With purple and with peacock fan,
Rested that merry gentleman;
And nothing him dismayed.

G. K. Chesterton

THE CHRISTMAS TREE

Put out the lights now!
Look at the Tree, the rough tree dazzled
In oriole plumes of flame,
Tinselled with twinkling frost fire, tasselled
With stars and moons — the same
That yesterday hid in the spinney and had no fame
Till we put out the lights now.

Hard are the nights now :
The fields at moonrise turn to agate,
Shadows are cold as jet;
In dyke and furrow, in copse and faggot
The frost's tooth is set;
And stars are the sparks whirled out by the north wind's fret
On the flinty nights now.

So feast your eyes now
On mimic star and moon-cold bauble :
Words may wither unseen,
But the Christmas Tree is a tree of fable,
A phoenix in evergreen,
And the world cannot change or chill what its mysteries
    mean
To your hearts and eyes now.

The vision dies now
Candle by candle : the tree that embraced it
Returns to its own kind,
To be earthed again and weather as best it
May the frost and the wind.
Children, it too had its hour — you will not mind
If it lives or dies now.

Cecil Day Lewis

From 'The Flight into Egypt' (Section III)

Well, so that is that. Now we must dismantle the tree,
    Putting the decorations back into their cardboard
        boxes —
    Some have got broken — and carrying them up to the
        attic.
    The holly and the mistletoe must be taken down and
        burnt,
And the children got ready for school. There are enough
Left-overs to do, warmed-up, for the rest of the week —
Not that we have much appetite, having drunk such a lot,
Stayed up so late, attempted — quite unsuccessfully —
To love all of our relatives, and in general
Grossly overestimated our powers. Once again
As in previous years, we have seen the actual Vision and
    failed
To do more than entertain it as an agreeable
Possibility, once again we have sent Him away,
Begging though to remain His disobedient servant,
The promising child who cannot keep His word for long.

                          W. H. Auden

VI

And let
the New Year
in

IV

And let
the New Year
in

NEW YEAR CAROL

Here we bring new water
    From the well so clear
For to worship God with
    This happy New Year.

Sing levy dew, levy dew,
    The water and the wine,
The seven bright gold wires
    And the bugles that do shine.

Sing reign of Fair Maid,
    With gold upon her toe —
Open you the west door
    And turn the Old Year go.

Sing reign of Fair Maid
    With gold upon her chin —
Open you the east door
    And let the New Year in.

Sing levy dew, levy dew,
    The water and the wine;
The seven bright gold wires
    And the bugles that do shine.

Anonymous

RING OUT THE OLD, RING IN THE NEW
from 'In Memoriam'

Ring out, wild bells, to the wild sky,
    The flying cloud, the frosty light;
    The year is dying in the night;
Ring out, wild bells, and let him die.

Ring out the old, ring in the new,
    Ring, happy bells, across the snow;
    The year is going, let him go;
Ring out the false, ring in the true. . . .

Ring out old shapes of foul disease;
    Ring out the narrowing lust of gold;
    Ring out the thousand wars of old,
Ring in the thousand years of peace.

Ring in the valiant man and free,
    The larger heart, the kindlier hand;
    Ring out the darkness of the land,
Ring in the Christ that is to be.

Alfred Lord Tennyson

TO THE NATIVITY

Evil flies the earth
now comfort is come :
God is on earth,
now earth is heaven.
Now the world is even
as the eternal Good
since in the Crib
all heaven is;
all that lacked to the glory
of earth is given :
God is on earth,
now earth is heaven.
Now Man He descends
that ye may rise;

now God and Man
one name unites.
Twixt heaven and earth
now the strife is striven:
God is on earth,
now earth is heaven.

Fernán González de Eslava, translated by Samuel Beckett

THE CIRCLE OF A GIRL'S ARMS
from 'The Reed'

The circle of a girl's arms
have changed the world
the round and sorrowful world
to a cradle for God.

She has laid love in His cradle.
In every cot,
Mary has laid her child.

In each
comes Christ.
In each Christ comes
to birth,
comes Christ from the Mother's breast,
as the bird from the sun
returning,
returning again to the tree he knows
and the nest,
to last year's rifled nest.

Into our hands
Mary has given her child,

heir to the world's tears,
heir to the world's toil,
heir to the world's scars,
heir to the chill dawn
over the ruin of wars.

She has laid love in His cradle,
answering for us all.
'Be it done unto me.'

The child in the wooden bed,
the light in the dark house,
the life in the failing soul,
the Host in the priest's hands,
the seed in the hard earth,
the man who is child again,
quiet in the burial bands
waiting his birth.

Mary, Mother of God,
we are the poor soil
and the dry dust,
we are hard with a cold frost.

Be warmth to the world,
be the thaw,
warm on the cold frost,
be the thaw that melts.
That the tender shoot of Christ,
piercing the hard heart,
flower to a spring in us.

Be hands that are rocking the world
to a kind rhythm of love;

that the incoherence of war
and the chaos of our unrest
be soothed to a lullaby,
and the round and sorrowful world
in your hands,
the cradle of God.

Caryll Houselander

JOY

'I have no name :
I am but two days old.'
What shall I call thee ?
'I happy am,
Joy is my name.'
Sweet joy befall thee!

Pretty joy!
Sweet joy, but two days old.
Sweet Joy I call thee.
Thou dost smile,
I sing the while,
Sweet joy befall thee!

William Blake

TO THE NAME ABOVE EVERY NAME, THE NAME OF JESUS

Come, lovely Name! appear from forth the bright
　　Regions of peaceful light.
Look from thine own illustrious home,
Fair King of Names, and come :
Leave all thy native glories in their gorgeous nest

97

And give thyself awhile the gracious guest
Of humble souls, that seek to find
     The hidden sweets
     Which man's heart meets
When thou art master of the mind.

Come, lovely name; life of our hope!
Lo, we hold our hearts wide ope!
Unlock thy cabinet of day,
Dearest sweet, and come away.
     Lo, how the thirsty lands
Gasp for thy golden showers! with long stretched hands
     Lo, how the labouring earth
     That hopes to be
     All heaven by thee,
     Leaps at thy birth!
The attending world, to wait thy rise,
     First turned to eyes;
And then, not knowing what to do,
Turned them to tears, and spent them too.

Come, royal name, and pay the expense
Of all this precious patience.
     O come away
And kill the death of this delay!
O see so many worlds of barren years
Melted and measured out in seas of tears.
O see the weary lids of wakeful hope
(Love's eastern windows) all wide ope
     With curtains drawn,
To catch the day-break of thy dawn.
O dawn at last, long-looked-for day!
Take thine own wings, and come away. . . .

Welcome, dear all-adored Name!
For sure, there is no knee
That knows not thee.
Or if there be such sons of shame
    Alas what will they do
     When stubborn rocks shall bow
And hills hang down their heaven-saluting heads
    To seek for humble beds
Of dust, where in the bashful shades of night,
Next to their own low nothing, they may lie,
And couch before the dazzling light of thy dread majesty.
They that by love's mild dictate now
    Will not adore thee,
Shall then with just confusion bow
    And break before thee.

Richard Crashaw

IESU

Iesu is in my heart, his sacred name
Is deeply carved there; but the other week
A great affliction broke the little frame,
Even all to pieces : which I went to seek :
And first I found the corner where was I,
After where ES, the next where U was graved.
When I had got these parcels, instantly
I sat me down to spell them, and perceived,
That to my broken heart he was *I ease you*,
           And to my whole is IESU.

George Herbert

A BABE IS BORN

A babe is born all of a may
    To bring salvation unto us.
To him we sing both night and day
    Veni creator Spiritus.

At Bethlehem, that blessed place,
    The child of bliss now born he was;
And him to serve God gave us grace,
    O lux beata Trinitas.

There came three kings out of the east
    To worship the king that is so free,
With gold and myrrh and frankincense,
    A solis ortus cardine.

The angels came down with one cry,
    A fair song that night sung they
In the worship of that child :
    Gloria tibi Domine.

Anonymous

JOURNEY OF THE MAGI

'A cold coming we had of it,
Just the worst time of the year
For a journey, and such a long journey :
The ways deep and the weather sharp,
The very dead of winter.'
And the camels galled, sore-footed, refractory,
Lying down in the melting snow.
There were times we regretted
The summer palaces on slopes, the terraces,

And the silken girls bringing sherbet.
Then the camel men cursing and grumbling
And running away, and wanting their liquor and women,
And the night-fires going out, and the lack of shelters,
And the cities hostile and the towns unfriendly
And the villages dirty and charging high prices:
A hard time we had of it.
At the end we preferred to travel all night,
Sleeping in snatches,
With the voices singing in our ears, saying
That this was all folly.

Then at dawn we came down to a temperate valley,
Wet, below the snow line, smelling of vegetation,
With a running stream and a water-mill beating the
        darkness,
And three trees on the low sky.
And an old white horse galloped away in the meadow.
Then we came to a tavern with vine-leaves over the lintel,
Six hands at an open door dicing for pieces of silver,
And feet kicking the empty wine-skins.
But there was no information, and so we continued
And arrived at evening, not a moment too soon
Finding the place; it was (you may say) satisfactory.

All this was a long time ago, I remember,
And I would do it again, but set down
This set down
This : were we led all that way for
Birth or Death? There was a Birth, certainly,
We had evidence and no doubt. I had seen birth and death,
But had thought they were different; this Birth was
Hard and bitter agony for us, like Death, our death.
We returned to our places, these Kingdoms,

But no longer at ease here, in the old dispensation,
With an alien people clutching their gods.
I should be glad of another death.

T. S. Eliot

I AM THE PRINCE

I am the Prince
I am the lowly
I am the damned
I am the holy.
My hands are ten knives.
I am the dove
Whose wings are murder.
My name is love.

Charles Causley

THE FLIGHT INTO EGYPT
from 'The Wakefield Cycle'

ANGEL   Awake, Joseph, and take good heed!
Arise and sleep no more!
If thou wilt save thyself indeed
Fast flee to foreign shore.
I am an angel at your need
Sent to shield you as decreed
And save from evils sore.
If not hence soon thou speed
For pity thou wilt plead
And mourn thy fate the more.

JOSEPH   God on his throne!
What wondrous deed
Yields so sweet tone?

102

ANGEL   No, Joseph, it is I,
            An angel sent to thee.

JOSEPH   Alas, I pray thee why?
            What is thy will with me?

ANGEL   Fast from here now hie,
            And take with thee Mary,
            And also her child so free;
            For Herod deems must die
            All boys born, surely,
            But yet of age that be
            Not two.

JOSEPH   Alas, full woe is me!
            What shall we do?

ANGEL   To Egypt shall thou fare
            With all the speed you may;
            And Joseph, bide you there
            Till otherwise I say.

JOSEPH   This is a sad affair
            For a man so old to bear,
            To feel such fear to stay.
            My bones are bruised and bare,
            Unfit to fare. Would it were
            My life's last day
            Come to an end.
            I know not which is the way.
            How shall we wend?

ANGEL   Thereof have thou no dread;
Go forth and cease thy din;
The Lord, where thou wilt tread,
Will guide thy steps from sin. . . .

JOSEPH   Now fails my strength, I fear,
And sight that I should see,
Mary, my darling dear,
I am full woe for thee!

MARY   Sweet Joseph now, what cheer?
To see you shed a tear
It truly troubles me.

JOSEPH   Our cares are coming near
If we dwell longer here;
Therefore we have to flee
Unseen.

MARY   Alas! how may this be?
Whatever may this mean?

JOSEPH   It means of sorrows a blight.

MARY   Ah, Joseph dear, how so?

JOSEPH   As I dreamt in the night,
As I turned to and fro,
An angel full of light,
As on bough is blossom bright,
Warned me of our woe:
How Herod in his spite
All boys born would affright
With death: he would also,

That fiend,
Thy son's life in his might
Most shamefully end.

MARY   My son? Alas, my care!
Who may my sorrows still?
Ill may false Herod fare.
My son why should he kill?
Alas, let's seek a lair,
This bairn I bore to snare
What worldly wretch had will? . . .

JOSEPH   Now, Mary dear, be still;
This helps us nought.
It is not well to weep
When weeping is in vain;
Our cares we still must keep,
And this makes more our pain.

MARY   The sorrows that I reap
That my sweet son asleep,
Is sought for to be slain.
Should I to Herod creep
I'd show my hatred deep.
Sweet Joseph, speak words plain
To me.

JOSEPH   Swift swaddle your son again
And his death flee.

MARY   His death would I not see
For all the world to win;
Alas, full woe were me,
Our bane should so begin;

105

My sweet child on my knee,
To slay him were pity,
And a foul heinous sin.
Dear Joseph, what say ye?

JOSEPH   To Egypt wend shall we;
Therefore let be thy din
And cry.

MARY   The way how shall we win?

JOSEPH   Full well know I. . . .

MARY   Alas, full woe is me!
None is so sad as I!
My heart will break in three,
My son to see him die.

JOSEPH   Ah, Mary love, let be,
And nothing dread for thee,
In haste hence let us hie;
To save thy lad so free,
Fast forth now let us flee,
Dear wife —
To meet his enemy
It were to lose our life.

And that will I not hear.
Away then we must be,
My heart would be full drear
You two apart to see.
To Egypt let us fare;
This pack till I come there

Thou leave me to carry.
Therefore have thou no care
My help I shall not spare
Thou wilt find no fault in me,
I say.

God bless this company,
And have now all good day!
Anonymous, edited by Martial Rose

AS MARY WAS A-WALKING

As Mary was a-walking
    By Bethlehem one day,
Her Son was in her arms,
    So heavenly to see.

'O give me water, Mother.'
    'You cannot drink, my dear;
For the rivers they are muddy,
    And the streams they are not clear;

'The rivers they are muddy,
    And the streams they are not clear,
And the springs are full of blood,
    You cannot drink from here.'

They came into a grove,
    So thick with oranges
That not another orange
    Could hang upon the trees;
There sat a man to guard them,
    Was blind in both his eyes.

'Give me an orange, blind man,
  To feed my Son today.'
'And take as many, lady,
  As you can bear away;

'Gather the biggest, lady,
  That most are to your mind,
The small ones soon will ripen,
  If you leave them behind.'

They gathered them by one and one,
  There grew a hundred more,
And straight the man began to see
  That had been blind before.

'O who is this fair lady,
  Has made me see again?'
It was the Holy Virgin
  That walked by Bethlehem.

Anonymous. Spanish ballad, translated by Edith C. Batho

BETHLEHEM

Oh ye, as shepherds or as kings,
That tread in hope this metalled way,
Think not to find again the cave
Where God Incarnate lay.

No breath of air from Shepherds' Fields,
No gleam of star, no glimpse of sky,
No sound of village life comes here,
No ox or ass stands by.

But high above us towers the church,
And there the warring factions keep
Continual strife about the place
Where Peace was wont to sleep.

The floor by pilgrim feet is worn,
The stones by fervent lips are pressed,
That love their God, but cannot love
His image manifest.

And, grim reminder of the past,
A policeman in the grotto stands,
Lest they who worship God with words
Offend Him with their hands,

In anger raised to strike the blow
That brands us with the curse of Cain,
And wakes a sleeping Child to weep
And take up His Cross again.

Phyllis Hartnoll

COME TO YOUR HEAVEN

This little babe so few days old,
Is come to rifle Satan's fold;
All hell doth at his presence quake,
Though he himself for cold do shake;
For in this weak unarmed wise
The gates of hell he will surprise.

With tears he fights and wins the field,
His naked breast stands for a shield,
His battering shot are babish cries,
His arrows, looks of weeping eyes.

His martial ensigns, cold and need,
And feeble flesh his warrior's steed.

His camp is pitched in a stall,
His bulwark but a broken wall,
The crib his trench, hay-stalks his stakes,
Of shepherds he his muster makes;
And thus, as sure his foe to wound,
The angels' trumps alarums sound.

Robert Southwell

TWELFTH NIGHT

Take down the gleaming holly and the pale
Mysterious mistletoe, the red and white;
And on the hearth where late the Yule-log flamed
Set all alight.

In cleansing fire burn up the vanished year.
The smoke shall bear away its joy and pain,
Its faults and follies and its dear delight,
Its loss and gain.

Feed the bright flame; now the dry crackling boughs
Shall yield repentant ash to strew the earth
That waits in silence and in solitude
For a new birth.

Phyllis Hartnoll

110

VII

Seek him in the kingdom of anxiety

From 'The Flight into Egypt' (Section IV)

He is the Way.
Follow him through the Land of Unlikeness;
You will see rare beasts, and have unique adventures.

He is the Truth.
Seek him in the Kingdom of Anxiety;
You will come to a great city that has expected your return
    for years.

He is the Life.
Love him in the World of the Flesh;
And at your marriage all its occasions shall dance for joy.

W. H. Auden

THE CARPENTER

Silent at Joseph's side He stood,
And smoothed and trimmed the shapeless wood,
And with firm hand, assured and slow,
Drove in each nail with measured blow.

Absorbed, He planned a wooden cask,
Nor asked for any greater task,
Content to make, with humble tools,
Tables and little children's stools.

Lord, give me careful hands to make
Such simple things as for Thy sake,
Happy within Thine house to dwell
If I may make one table well.

Phyllis Hartnoll

GOD ABIDES IN MEN

God abides in men,
because Christ has put on
the nature of man, like a garment,
and worn it to His own shape.
He has put on everyone's life.
He has fitted Himself to the little child's dress,
to the shepherd's coat of sheepskin,
to the workman's coat,
to the King's red robes,
to the snowy loveliness of the wedding garment,
and to the drab
of the sad, simple battle dress.

Christ has put on Man's nature,
and given him back his humanness,
worn to the shape
of limitless love,
and warm from the touch
of His life.

He has given man his crown,
the thorn that is jewelled
with drops of His blood.
He has given him
the seamless garment
of his truth.
He has bound him
in the swaddling bands
of his humility.
He has fastened his hands
to the tree of life.

114

He has latched his feet
in crimson sandals
that they move not
from the path of love.

God abides in man.

Caryll Houselander

THE ELIXIR

Teach me, my God and king,
  In all things thee to see,
And what I do in anything,
  To do it as for thee.

Not rudely, as a beast,
  To run into an action;
But still to make thee prepossessed,
  And give it his perfection.

A man that looks on glass,
  On it may stay his eye;
Or if he pleases, through it pass,
  And then the heaven espy. . . .

A servant with this clause
  Makes drudgery divine;
Who sweeps a room, as for thy laws,
  Makes that and the action fine.

This is the famous stone
  That turneth all to gold;
For that which God doth touch and own
  Cannot for less be told.

George Herbert

MARTHA OF BETHANY

It's all very well
Sitting in the shade of the courtyard
Talking about your souls.
Someone's got to see to the cooking,
Standing at the oven all the morning
With you two taking your ease.
It's all very well
Saying he'd be content
With bread and honey.
Perhaps he would — but I wouldn't,
Coming to our house like this,
Not giving him of our best.
Yes, it's all very well
Him trying to excuse you,
Saying your recipe's best,
Saying I worry too much,
That I'm always anxious.
Someone's got to worry —
And double if the others don't care.
For it's all very well
Talking of faith and belief,
But what would you do
If everyone sat in the cool
Not getting their meals?
And he can't go wandering and preaching
On an empty stomach —
He'd die in the first fortnight.
Then where would you be
With all your discussions and questions
And no one to answer them?
It's all very well.

Clive Sansom

WORK

There is no point in work
unless it absorbs you
like an absorbing game.

If it doesn't absorb you
if it's never any fun,
don't do it. . . .

D. H. Lawrence

THE PAINTER'S PHILOSOPHY
from 'Fra Lippo Lippi'

      'You've seen the world
— The beauty and the wonder and the power,
The shapes of things, their colours, lights and shades,
Changes, surprises — and God made it all!
For what? Do you feel thankful, ay or no,
For this fair town's face, yonder river's line,
The mountain round it and the sky above,
Much more the figures of man, woman, child,
These are the frame to? What's it all about?
To be passed over, despised? or dwelt upon,
Wondered at? oh, this last of course! — you say.
But why not do as well as say — paint these
Just as they are, careless what comes of it?
God's works — paint any one, and count it crime
To let a truth slip. Don't object 'His works
Are here already; nature is complete :
Suppose you reproduce her — (which you can't) —
There's no advantage! you must beat her, then!'
For, don't you mark? we're made so that we love
First when we see them painted, things we have passed

Perhaps a hundred times nor cared to see;
And so they are better, painted — better to us,
Which is the same thing. Art was given for that;
God uses us to help each other so,
Lending our minds out. Have you noticed, now,
Your cullion's hanging face? A bit of chalk,
And trust me but you should, though! How much more
If I drew higher things with the same truth!
That were to take the Prior's pulpit place,
Interpret God to all of you! Oh, oh,
It makes me mad to see what men shall do
And we in our graves! This world's no blot for us,
Nor blank; it means intensely, and means good :
To find its meaning is my meat and drink.'

Robert Browning

From 'Sext', No. 3 from 'Horae Canonicae'

You need not see what someone is doing
to know if it is his vocation,

you have only to watch his eyes :
a cook mixing a sauce, a surgeon

making a primary incision,
a clerk completing a bill of lading,

wear the same rapt expression,
forgetting themselves in a function.

How beautiful it is,
that eye-on-the-object look.

W. H. Auden

Lord, Thou hast made this world below the shadow of a
    dream,
An', taught by time, I tak' it so — exceptin' always Steam.
From coupler-flange to spindle-guide I see Thy Hand, O
    God —
Predestination in the stride o' yon connectin'-rod.
John Calvin might ha' forged the same — enorrmous,
    certain, slow —
Ay, wrought it in the furnace-flame — *my* 'Institutio'.
I cannot get my sleep tonight; old bones are hard to please;
I'll stand the middle watch up here — alone wi' God an'
    these
My engines, after ninety days o' race an' rack an' strain
Through all the seas of all Thy world, slam-bangin' home
    again.
Slam-bang too much — they knock a wee — the crosshead-
    gibs are loose,
But thirty thousand mile o' sea has gied them fair excuse....

That minds me of our Viscount loon — Sir Kenneth's kin —
    the chap
Wi' Russia leather tennis-shoon an' spar-decked yachtin'
    cap.
I showed him round last week, o'er all — an' at the last
    says he:
'Mister M'Andrew, don't you think steam spoils romance
    at sea?'
Damned ijjit! I'd been doon that morn to see what ailed the
    throws,
Manholin', on my back — the cranks three inches off my
    nose.
Romance! Those first-class passengers they like it very
    well,

Printed an' bound in little books; but why don't poets tell?
I'm sick of all their quirks an' turns — the loves an' doves
they dream —
Lord, send a man like Robbie Burns to sing the Song o'
Steam!
To match wi' Scotia's noblest speech yon orchestra sublime
Whaurto — uplifted like the Just — the tail-rods mark the
time.
The crank-throws give the double-bass, the feed-pump sobs
an' heaves,
An' now the main eccentrics start their quarrel on the
sheaves:
Her time, her own appointed time, the rocking link-head
bides,
Till — hear that note? — the rod's return whings glim-
merin' through the guides.
They're all awa'! True beat, full power, the clangin' chorus
goes
Clear to the tunnel where they sit, my purrin' dynamoes.
Interdependence absolute, foreseen, ordained, decreed,
To work, Ye'll note, at ony tilt an' every rate o' speed.
Fra' skylight-lift to furnace-bars, backed, bolted, braced an'
stayed,
An' singin' like the Mornin' Stars for joy that they are
made;
While, out o' touch o' vanity, the sweatin' thrust-block
says:
'Not unto us the praise, or man — not unto us the praise!'
Now, a' together, hear them lift their lesson — theirs an'
mine:
'Law, Orrder, Duty an' Restraint, Obedience, Discipline!'
Mill, forge an' try-pit taught them that when roarin' they
arose,
An' whiles I wonder if a soul was gied them wi' the blows.
Oh for a man to weld it then, in one trip-hammer strain,

Till even first-class passengers could tell the meanin' plain!
But no one cares except mysel' that serve an' understand
My seven thousand horse-power here. Eh, Lord! They're
     grand — they're grand!
Uplift am I? When first in store the new-made beasties
     stood,
Were Ye cast down that breathed the Word declarin' all
     things good?
Not so! O' that warld-liftin' joy no after-fall could vex,
Ye've left a glimmer still to cheer the Man — the Arrtifex!
That holds, in spite o' knock an' scale, o' friction, waste an'
     slip,
An' by that light — now, mark my word — we'll build the
     Perfect Ship.
I'll never last to judge her lines or take her curve — not I.
But I ha' lived an' I ha' worked. Be thanks to Thee, Most
     High!'

Rudyard Kipling

FRENCH PEASANTS

These going home at dusk
Along the lane,
After the day's warm work,
Do not complain.

Were you to say to them
'What does it mean?
What is it all about,
This troubled dream?'

They would not understand,
They'd go their way,

Or, if they spoke at all,
They'd surely say,

'Dawn is the time to rise,
Days are to earn
Bread and the mid-day rest,
Dusk to return;

'To be content, to pray,
To hear songs sung,
Or to make wayside love,
If one is young.

'All from the good God comes,
All then is good;
Sorrow is known to Him,
And understood.'

One who had questioned all,
And was not wise,
Might be ashamed to meet
Their quiet eyes.

All is so clear to them,
All is so plain,
Those who go home at dusk,
Along the lane.

Monk Gibbon

CYNDDYLAN ON A TRACTOR

Ah, you should see Cynddylan on a tractor.
Gone the old look that yoked him to the soil;
He's a new man now, part of the machine,
His nerves of metal and his blood oil.
The clutch curses, but the gears obey
His least bidding, and lo, he's away
Out of the farmyard, scattering hens.
Riding to work now as a great man should,
He is the knight at arms breaking the fields'
Mirror of silence, emptying the wood
Of foxes and squirrels and bright jays.
The sun comes over the tall trees
Kindling all the hedges, but not for him
Who runs his engine on a different fuel.
And all the birds are singing, bills wide in vain,
As Cynddylan passes proudly up the lane.

R. S. Thomas

FISH CRIER

I know a Jew fish crier down on Maxwell Street with a
voice like a north wind blowing over corn stubble in
January.
He dangles herring before prospective customers evincing
a joy identical with that of Pavlova dancing.
His face is that of a man terribly glad to be selling fish,
terribly glad that God made fish, and customers to
whom he may call his wares from a pushcart.

Carl Sandburg

JOHN HENRY

Captain said to John Henry
'Gonna bring me a steam drill round.
Gonna take that steam drill out on the job,
Gonna whop that steel on down.'

John Henry told his captain,
Lightnin' was in his eye:
'I'll never be conquered by your old steam drill,
I'll beat it to the bottom or I'll die.'

John Henry walked in the tunnel,
Had his captain by his side.
But the rock so tall, John Henry so small,
Lord, he laid down his hammer, an' he cried.

Now John Henry start on the right hand,
An' the steam drill start on the left.
'Before I let this steam drill beat me down,
I'll hammer myself to death.'

Well, John Henry kissed his hammer,
The white man turned on the steam;
Little Bill held John Henry's trusty steel;
Was the biggest race the world ever seen.

John Henry said as he took his stand:
'This'll be the end of me.'
But every foot that steam drill drove
John Henry's hammer drove three.

John Henry was hammerin' on the mountain,
An' his hammer was strikin' fire.
He drove so hard till he broke his heart,
An' he lay down his hammer an' he died.

When John Henry died there wasn't no box
Big enough to hold his bones.
So they buried him in a box-car deep in the ground,
Let two mountains be his gravestones.

An' they took John Henry from the graveyard,
An' buried him away in the sand,
An' every locomotive comes roarin' by
Whistles : 'There lies a steel-drivin' man'.

Anonymous. American Folk Song

SPACE PILOT

The land sinks back,
The rockets shoot their bolt,
Earth's pull weakens and dies.
I breach space and become a celestial body,
Moving with planets and suns
Through darkness, silence and cold,
But having no place in this void,
My weight lost, my breath in an envelope,
My eyes replaced by intricate instruments,
There is no place for the heart
Here, needing the light and seasons.
But the soul perhaps ?
Released from all that I could not carry with me
I shall stare unhindered into the face of God.

John Blackie

A SONG OF KABIR

O Friend, hope for him whilst you live, know whilst you
       live, understand whilst you live;
For in life deliverance abides.
If your bonds be not broken whilst living,
What hope of deliverance in death?

It is but an empty dream that the soul shall have union with
       him because it has passed from the body.
If he is found now, he is found then;
If not, we do but go to dwell in the City of Death.
    Rabindranath Tagore, translated by Evelyn Underhill

THE PARDON
from 'Piers Plowman', Passus VII

Truth heard tell of this and told the Plowman
To take his team and till his acre,
And provide him a pardon, *a poena et a culpa*,
For him and for his heirs forever after.
He bade him hold himself at home and harrow his acre;
And all who helped in harrowing, or in sowing or setting,
Or in any other means that might aid their master,
Should have pardon with Piers Plowman, as Truth has
    granted. . . .

Whoever is old and hoary and helpless and strengthless,
And women with child, who are unfit for working,
The blind and the bed-rid and all with broken members,
And all patient poor folk, lepers and others,
Shall have as perfect a pardon as the Plowman himself. . . .

Piers opened his pardon at the priest's bidding.
I was behind them both and beheld all the charter.
All lay in two lines, and not a leaf further.
The witness was Truth; and it was written thus:
Et qui bona egerunt, ibunt in vitam eternam.
Qui vero mala, in ignem eternum.

'Peter,' said the priest, 'there is no pardon in it,
But do well and have well, and God shall have your soul,
And do evil and have evil, and you may hope only
That after your death day the devil shall take you.'

   William Langland, translated by H. W. Wells

THE KINGDOM OF GOD

'In no strange land'

O world invisible, we view thee,
O world intangible, we touch thee,
O world unknowable, we know thee,
Inapprehensible, we clutch thee!

Does the fish soar to find the ocean,
The eagle plunge to find the air —
That we ask of the stars in motion
If they have rumour of thee there?

Not where the wheeling systems darken,
And our benumbed conceiving soars! —
The drift of pinions, would we hearken,
Beats at our own clay-shuttered doors.

The angels keep their ancient places; —
Turn but a stone, and start a wing!
'Tis ye, 'tis your estranged faces
That miss the many-splendoured thing.

But (when so sad thou canst not sadder)
Cry; — and upon thy so sore loss
Shall shine the traffic of Jacob's ladder
Pitched betwixt Heaven and Charing Cross.

Yea, in the night, my Soul, my daughter,
Cry, — clinging heaven by the hems;
And lo, Christ walking on the water,
Not of Genesareth, but Thames!

Francis Thompson

Are there anybody here like Mary a-weeping?

VIII

Are there
anybody here
like
Mary
a-weeping?

I AM THE GREAT SUN
(*from a Norman crucifix of 1632*)

I am the great sun, but you do not see me,
    I am your husband, but you turn away.
I am the captive, but you do not free me,
    I am the captain you will not obey.

I am the truth, but you will not believe me,
    I am the city where you will not stay,
I am your wife, your child, but you will leave me,
    I am that God to whom you will not pray.

I am your counsel, but you do not hear me,
    I am that lover whom you will betray,
I am the victor, but you do not cheer me,
    I am the holy dove whom you will slay.

I am your life, but if you will not name me,
Seal up your soul with tears, and never blame me.

Charles Causley

PREPARATIONS

Yet if his Majesty, our sovereign lord,
Should of his own accord
Friendly himself invite,
And say 'I'll be your guest tomorrow night',
How should we stir ourselves, call and command
All hands to work! 'Let no man idle stand!

'Set me fine Spanish tables in the hall,
See they be fitted all;
Let there be room to eat
And order taken that there want no meat.
See every sconce and candlestick made bright,
That without tapers they may give a light.

'Look to the presence : are the carpets spread,
The dazie o'er the head,
The cushions in the chairs,
And all the candles lighted on the stairs?
Perfume the chambers, and in any case
Let each man give attendance in his place!'

Thus, if the king were coming, would we do;
And 'twere good reason, too;
For 'tis a duteous thing
To show all honour to an earthly king,
And after all our travail and our cost,
So he be pleased, to think no labour lost.

But at the coming of the King of Heaven,
All's set at six and seven;
We wallow in our sin,
Christ cannot find a chamber in the inn.
We entertain him always like a stranger,
And, as at first, still lodge him in the manger.

Anonymous

MEDITATIO

When I carefully consider the curious habits of dogs
I am compelled to conclude
That man is the superior animal.

When I consider the curious habits of man
I confess, my friend, I am puzzled.

Ezra Pound

THE POISON TREE

I was angry with my friend :
I told my wrath, my wrath did end.
I was angry with my foe :
I told it not, my wrath did grow.

And I watered it in fears,
Night and morning with my tears;
And I sunned it with smiles,
And with soft deceitful wiles.

And it grew both day and night,
Till it bore an apple bright;
And my foe beheld it shine,
And he knew that it was mine,

And into my garden stole
When the night had veiled the pole :
In the morning glad I see
My foe outstretched beneath the tree.

William Blake

THE DIGNITY OF MAN

Remember how God hath made thee reasonable
Like unto his image and figure,
And for thee suffered pains intolerable
That he for angel never would endure.
Regard, O man, thine excellent nature,
Thou that with angel art made to be equal,
For very shame be not the devil's thrall.

Thomas More

THE DAY OF WRATH

Day of the king most righteous,
 The day is nigh at hand,
The day of wrath and vengeance,
 And darkness on the land.

Day of thick clouds and voices,
 Of mighty thundering,
A day of narrow anguish
 And bitter sorrowing.

The love of women's over,
 And ended is desire,
Men's strife with men is quiet,
 And the world lusts no more.

St. Columba, translated by Helen Waddell

O SINNERMAN

O sinnerman, where are you going to run to,
            all on that day?
Run to the moon: O moon, won't you hide me,
            all on that day?
The Lord said: O sinnerman, the moon'll be a-bleeding,
            all on that day.

O sinnerman, where are you going to run to,
            all on that day?
Run to the stars: O stars, won't you hide me,
            all on that day?
The Lord said: O sinnerman, the stars'll be a-falling
            all on that day.

O sinnerman, where are you going to run to,
            all on that day?
Run to the rocks: O rocks won't you hide me,
            all on that day?
The Lord said: O sinnerman, the rocks'll be a-rolling
            all on that day.

Anonymous. Spiritual

HAUKYN'S COAT
from 'Piers Plowman', Passus XIII and XIV

He had a coat of Christendom as Holy Church teaches,
But it was marked in many places with many patches,
A patch there from pride, and there a patch of mad speaking,
Of scorning and of scoffing and of unschooled arrogance,
As pride among people in apparel and bearing.
He is willing that all men should hold him what he is not.
He shows himself otherwise than as his heart warrants. . . .

'By Christ,' said Conscience, 'your best coat, Haukyn,
Has many spots and mendings and must be well washed.'
'Yes, if you will take heed', said Haukyn, 'in all parts of it,
By the back and by the belly and by the sides also
You will find many folds and foul patches.'
Then he turned about quickly and I took good heed
That it was a far fouler coat than I had first thought it. . . .

'I have but one whole suit,' said Haukyn, 'I am the less
        blameworthy
If it is soiled and seldom clean; I sleep in it also. . . .
I have washed it in Lent and out of Lent often
With the wondrous soap of sickness that sinks so deeply;
And after the loss of goods I have been loath to injure
God or any good man, by aught that I could know of.
I shrived myself to the priest, who gave me against my
        sinning
The penance of patience and to give poor men nourishment;
And so for the sake of my Christianity to keep it cleanly.
But I could never, by Christ, keep it an hour
Without soiling it with some sight or with some idle
        speaking.
Either through words or works or the will within me
I slobbered and stained it from sunrise to even.'

'I shall tell you,' quoth Conscience, 'how contrition is
        possible,
And that will card your coat of all kinds of filthiness. . . .
Do-well will wash it and wring it through a wise con-
        fessor. . . .
Do-bet will cleanse it and beat it as bright as any scarlet,
And dye it in the grain with good will and with God's
        grace for amendment,
And so send you to satisfaction, and sew the pieces together,

136

Satisfactio, Do-best.
No mist will mar nor any moth corrupt it,
Nor any fiend or false man defile it in your lifetime;
No herald or harper will have a fairer garment
Than Haukyn the Active Man if you act by my teaching.'
          William Langland, translated by H. W. Wells

A HYMN TO GOD THE FATHER

Wilt thou forgive that sin where I begun,
    Which was my sin, though it were done before?
Wilt thou forgive that sin through which I run,
    And do run still, though still I do deplore?
        When thou hast done, thou hast not done,
            For I have more.

Wilt thou forgive that sin which I have won
    Others to sin, and made my sin their door?
Wilt thou forgive that sin which I did shun
    A year, or two, but wallowed in a score?
        When thou hast done, thou hast not done
            For I have more.

I have a sin of fear, that when I have spun
    My last thread, I shall perish on the shore;
But swear by thyself, that at my death thy sun
    Shall shine as he shines now, and heretofore;
        And having done that, thou hast done,
            I fear no more.
                                        John Donne

THE LAMP

For like a child sent with a fluttering light
To feel his way along a gusty night
Man walks the world : again and yet again
The lamp shall be by fits of passion slain :
But shall not he who sent him from the door
Relight the lamp once more and yet once more ?

Edward Fitzgerald

LOVE BADE ME WELCOME

Love bade me welcome, yet my soul drew back,
    Guilty of dust and sin.
But quick-eyed love, observing me grow slack
    From my first entrance in,
Drew nearer to me, sweetly questioning
    If I lacked anything.

'A guest,' I answered, 'worthy to be here'.
    Love said, 'You shall be he.'
'I, the unkind, ungrateful ? Ah, my dear,
    I cannot look on thee.'
Love took my hand, and smiling did reply,
    'Who made the eyes but I ?'

'Truth, Lord, but I have marred them : let my shame
    Go where it doth deserve'.
'And know you not,' says Love, 'who bore the blame ?'
    'My dear, then I will serve.'
'You must sit down,' says Love, 'and taste my meat.'
    So I did sit and eat.

George Herbert

From 'Songs between the Soul and the Bridegroom'

> My spirit I prepare
> To serve him with her riches and her beauty.
> No flocks are now my care,
> No other toil I share,
> And only now in loving is my duty.
>
> So now if from this day
> I am not found among the haunts of men,
> Say that I went astray
> Love-stricken from my way,
> That I was lost, but have been found again.
> *St. John of the Cross*, translated by Roy Campbell

CONFESSION — GATE OF PURGATORY
from 'Il Purgatorio', Canto IX

I saw a gate : three steps beneath it, each
  Of different hue, led upward; and thereat
  A porter, who as yet vouchsafed no speech.

Widening my eyes, I saw him, how he sat
  Over the topmost step, in countenance
  Such as would not abide the looking-at.

A naked sword was in his hand, whose dance
  Of mirrored rays so blinding blazed and shot,
  I tried and tried, but could not fix my glance. . . .

And when we reached the first step of the stair,
  It was white marble, polished to such glass
  That even as I am, I saw me there;

And dyed more dark than perse the second was —
    A calcined stone, rugged and rough in grain,
    And it was cracked both lengthways and across;

The third step, piled above the other twain,
    Seemed all of porphyry that flamed and shone
    Redder than bright blood spurting from a vein,

And this, God's Angel held both feet upon,
    And on the threshold of the door he sate,
    And that seemed made of adamantine stone. . . .

One golden and one silver key he had;
    With the white first, the yellow afterward,
    He wrought so with the gate that I was glad.

'Should one or other of the keys stick hard,
    Turning askew so that the tumblers block,'
    He said, 'this wicket cannot be unbarred.

'One's costlier; the other needs good stock
    Of wit and skill to get the bolt to stir,
    For that one grips the wards and frees the lock.

'From Peter hold I these, who bade me err
    In opening rather than in keeping fast,
    So men but kneeled to me without demur.'

The blest gate's door he pushed then, saying at last:
    'Enter; but I must warn you: back outside
    He goes, who looks behind him once he's passed.'
        Dante Alighieri, translated by Dorothy Sayers

ASH WEDNESDAY

Ashen cross traced on brow!
Iron cross hid in breast!
Have power, bring patience, now:
Bid passion be at rest.

O sad, dear, days of Lent!
Now lengthen your gray hours
If so we may repent,
Before the time of flowers.

Majestical, austere,
The sanctuaries look stern:
All silent! all severe!
Save where the lone lamps burn.

Imprisoned there above
The world's indifferency;
Still waits eternal love
With wounds from Calvary.

Come, mourning companies;
Come, to sad Christ draw near;
Come, sin's confederacies;
Lay down your malice here.

Here is the healing place,
And here the place of peace;
Sorrow is sweet with grace
Here, and here sin doth cease.

Lionel Johnson

WEEPING MARY

Are there anybody here like Mary a-weeping?
>   Call to my Jesus and he'll draw nigh.
Are there anybody here like Peter a-sinking?
>   Call to my Jesus and he'll draw nigh.
Glory, glory, glory, glory,
>   Glory be to my God on high.

>   *Anonymous. Spiritual*

TO HEAVEN

>   Open thy gates
> To him, who weeping waits,
>   And might come in,
> But that held back by sin.
>   Let mercy be
> So kind, to set me free,
>   And I will straight
> Come in, or force the gate.

>   *Robert Herrick*

ASH WEDNESDAY

Richt early on Ash Wednesday
Drinkin' the wine sat cummers tway;
    The tane did to the tither complain,
Sighin' an' sowpin' did she say —
    '*This lang Lenten mak's me lean.*'

On stool beside the fire she sat;
Gude kens if she was grit an' fat;
  Yet to be feeble she did feign,
And aye she said 'Here's proof o' that;
  It's the lang Lenten mak's me lean.'

'My fair sweet cummer,' quo' the tither,
'Ye tak' your leanness aff your mither.
  A' kind o' wine she would disdain
But malvaisie — she'd bide nae ither.'
  This lang Lenten mak's me lean.

'Cummer, be blithe, baith e'en an' morrow,
An' let your husband drie the sorrow;
  But you from fasting should refrain;
And I'se uphaud, St. Bride to borrow,
  That Lenten shall not mak' you lean.'

'Your counsel, cummer, 's gude,' quo' she;
'Fill a fu' cup and drink to me;
  That man of mine's no' worth a bean;
This is the only joy I ha'e,
  And Lenten shall not mak' me lean.'

This twa, out of a mutchkin stoup,
They drank twa chappin, sowp for sowp,
  Sae great a drouth did them constrain;
By then to mend they had gude howp,
  And Lenten wouldna mak' them lean.
  William Dunbar, modernised by H. **Haliburton**

IN THE WILDERNESS

He, of his gentleness,
Thirsting and hungering
Walked in the wilderness;
Soft words of grace he spoke
Unto lost desert-folk
That listened wondering.
He heard the bittern call
From ruined palace-wall,
Answered him brotherly.
He held communion
With the she-pelican
Of lonely piety.
Basilisk, cockatrice,
Flocked to his homilies,
With mail of dread device,
With monstrous barbed stings,
With eager dragon-eyes;
Great bats on leathern wings,
And old, blind, broken things,
Mean in their miseries.
Then ever with him went
Of all his wanderings
Comrade, with ragged coat,
Gaunt ribs — poor innocent —
Bleeding foot, burning throat,
The guileless young scape-goat:
For forty nights and days
Followed in Jesus' ways,
Sure guard behind him kept,
Tears like a lover wept.

Robert Graves

144

TO GOD

Lord, I am like to mistletoe,
Which has no root, and cannot grow
Or prosper, but by that same tree
It clings about; so I by thee.
What need I then to fear at all
So long as I about thee crawl?
But if that tree should fall and die,
Tumble shall heaven, and down will I.

Robert Herrick

SONNET

I am not moved to love thee, my Lord God,
by the heaven thou hast promised me;
I am not moved by the sore dreaded hell
to forbear me from offending thee.

I am moved by thee, Lord; I am moved
at seeing thee nailed upon the cross and mocked;
I am moved by thy body all over wounds;
I am moved by thy dishonour and thy death.

I am moved, last, by thy love, in such a wise
that though there were no heaven I still should love thee,
and though there were no hell I still should fear thee.

I need no gift of thee to make me love thee;
for though my present hope were all despair,
as now I love thee I should love thee still.

Miguel de Guevara, translated by Samuel Beckett

MAN LOOK NOT BACK

Man, look not back — it would be but to see
How crooked is the furrow ploughed by thee.

Anonymous

THE SPIRITUAL RAILWAY

The line to heaven by us is made,
With heavenly truth the rails are laid;
From earth to heaven the line extends
And in eternal life it ends.

Repentance is the station,
Where passengers are taken in;
No fee for them is there to pay,
For love is in itself the way.

God's word is the first engineer,
It points the way to heaven so clear;
Through tunnels dark and dreary there
It does the way to glory steer.

God's love the fire, his grace the steam
Which drives the engine and the train.
All you who would to glory ride
Must come to God, in him abide.

Come then, poor sinners, now's the time,
At any station on the line;
If you'll repent and turn from sin,
The train will stop, and take you in.

Anonymous

DONE FOUND MY LOST SHEEP

Done found my lost sheep, done found my lost sheep,
Done found my lost sheep,
                    Hallelujah!
I done found my lost sheep, done found my lost sheep,
Done found my lost sheep.

> My lord had a hundred sheep,
> One of them did go astray.
> That just left him ninety-nine.
> Go to the wilderness, seek and find,
> If you find him, bring him back,
> Cross the shoulders, cross your back.
> Tell the neighbours all around,
> That lost sheep has done been found.

Done found my lost sheep, done found my lost sheep,
Done found my lost sheep.

> In that resurrection day,
> Sinner can't find no hiding place.
> Go to the mountain, the mountain move.
> Run to the hill, the hill run too.
> Sinnerman travelling on trembling ground,
> Poor lost sheep ain't never been found.
> Sinner, why don't you stop and pray,
> Then you'd hear the shepherd say —

Done found my lost sheep, done found my lost sheep,
Done found my lost sheep.

                              Anonymous. Spiritual

ALL OTHER LOVE IS LIKE THE MOON

All other love is like the moon
That waxes and wanes like the flower of the plain,
Like the flower that faireth and fadeth soon,
As the day that showers and ends in rain.

All other love begins by bliss,
In weep and woe makes its ending,
No other love is for our peace
But that which rests in Heaven's King.

Whose love is springing, ever green,
And ever full, without waning;
Whose love is sweet, without pain,
Love without end, a perfect ring.

Anonymous. 14th Century

IX

Nineteen hundred and forty nails

THE CONQUEROR

In his one hand are pearls;
>A sword is in the other —
>>He that now thy door has broken.

He came not to beg
>But out of strife and conquest
>Thy soul to bear away —
>>He that now thy door has broken.

Along the road of Death
>Into thy life he came —
>>He that now thy door has broken.

Never will he go with half!
>Of all thou art he will
>Be absolute, sole Lord! —
>>He that now thy door has broken.

Rabindranath Tagore

PALM SUNDAY

Hark! how the children shrill and high
>*Hosanna* cry,
Their joys provoke the distant sky,
Where thrones and seraphims reply,
And their own angels shine and sing
>In a bright ring :
>Such young, sweet mirth
>Makes heaven and earth
Join in a joyful symphony.

Henry Vaughan

THE DONKEY'S OWNER

Snaffled my donkey, he did — good luck to him! —
Rode him astride, feet dangling, near scraping the ground.
Gave me the laugh of my life when I first see them,
Remembering yesterday — you know, how Pilate come
Bouncing along the same road, only that horse of his
Big as a bloody house and the armour shining
And half Rome trotting behind. Tight-mouthed he was,
Looking he owned the world.

                    Then today,
Him and my little donkey! Ha! — laugh? —
I thought I'd kill myself when he first started.
So did the rest of them. Gave him a cheer
Like he was Caesar himself, only more hearty :
Tore off some palm-twigs and followed shouting,
Whacking the donkey's behind. . . . Then suddenly
We see his face.
The smile had gone, and somehow the way he sat
Was different — like he was much older — you know —
Didn't want to laugh no more.

Clive Sansom

RIDE ON IN MAJESTY

Ride on! ride on in majesty!
In lowly pomp ride on to die;
O Christ, thy triumphs now begin
O'er captive death and conquered sin.

Ride on! ride on in majesty!
Thy winged squadrons of the sky
Look down with sad and wondering eyes
To see the approaching sacrifice.

Ride on! ride on in majesty!
The last and fiercest strife is nigh;
The father on his sapphire throne
Awaits his own anointed son.

Henry Hart Milman

THE DREAM OF THE ROOD

Lo, I will tell you the best of dreams,
What I dreamt at midnight
When men with their voices were at rest:

I thought I saw the strangest tree
Climbing the sky, wound round with light:
The brightest shaft in the world,
A beacon drenched in gold;
A wonder of the night!

Gems shone fair on the earth below
And there were five jewels up on the shoulder-bough:
All the angels of God, eternal in beauty,
Behold it now.

O this is no gallows for a thief condemned
For good men on earth look thither with love,
All this created wonder, the world, sees it,
And the holy spirits above.

It is a tree of victory blazing on me
And my sin is foul before it:
I am wounded with infirmity:

I saw the glorious sign
Honoured with vestures, blissful shine,

153

And there seemed as gold cast o'er it,
And gems decked worthily the Ruler's Tree.

But beneath all the gold
I could see the trace of an old struggle and sad
When the right side sweat blood — O my heart swelled
    with trouble,
I was afraid of that glistering thing!

Then the swift beacon changed its glory,
Lost its fair look. I saw it stream cold,
Running with sweat of blood. — Then again it was a
    treasure
Of chosen gold.

So there I lay with ruth in my heart
On and on, watching the Healer's tree
Till it spoke! Till I heard that most precious wood
Sound words in the silence :
'It was long since : they hewed me low
(But I remember!) in the forest-row.
They plucked me from my rooted heart,
Strong enemies, and by base art
Mismade me in a shape of scorn
And bid me swing their knaves unborn!
On men's shoulders I rode at last
To a little hill. Foes made me fast.

Then I saw the Lord of man
Press on to climb me!
I dare not bend against command
Of the Lord, though I saw the land
Quiver and shudder in its clay.
I could throw down all his foes

154

But I held fast.
                    Heroic, fair,
The young knight who was God made bare
His breast. He was ready then,
In the sight of many, to ransom men.
He climbed the gallows, and he gave
No second thought, being sure and brave.
I shuddered when he clutched me round;
Flinch I dare not or fall to ground :
I was raised a cross, and it was I
Who swung an Emperor gallows-high :
The Lord of Heaven;
I durst not bow.

They drove dark nails through my side,
Open wounds of malice that abide
To be seen upon me. I durst not spurn
Our foes mocking us with hate and scorn.
I was wet with blood fallen from the man's breast
When soul went out, a wavering guest.
On that little hill I have overlived and borne
Cruel deeds. I saw stretched out and torn
Woeful, the Lord of Hosts.

Darkness has masked the falling day,
Our Healer's body bloodless lay
Stretched on the gallows, the weak rain
Wraps round and hides. This world of pain
With all creation, cries its loss,
The fall of a king :
Christ is on the cross!
See, come from far, each man of good
Draws near the prince. And I, the Rood,
In sorrow, humbly to the sod

155

Bowed down. They took Almighty God
Out of hard pain. Limbweary lay
His corpse fallen on earth. But they
Stood at his head and beheld God
Who rested, lying spent after the great fight.
Before my sight — his slayer's sight —
They shaped the coffin of brightest stone.
They entombed the Lord
And in dusk, sorrowful,
Raised a mourning song.

They left me steamed with sweat,
With arrows hasped, with wounds o'erset:
We three stayed weeping
For his body, fair house of life grown cold.
We were hacked down —
Thrust in a pit. But his disciples found me,
His friends — in silver they wound me,
Wrapped me in gold.'

Anonymous. Anglo-Saxon, translated by *Gavin Bone*

A DIVINE IMAGE

Cruelty has a human heart
And Jealousy a human face;
Terror the human form divine,
And Secrecy the human dress.

The human dress is forged iron,
The human form a fiery forge,
The human face a furnace sealed,
The human heart its hungry gorge.

William Blake

156

AN ARGUMENT—
OF THE PASSION OF CHRIST

Seeds of the three hours' agony
Fell on good earth, and grew from me,
And, cherished by my sleepless cares,
Flowered with God's Blood and Mary's tears.
My curious love found its reward
When Love was scourged in Pilate's yard :
Here was the work my hands had made :
A thorny crown, to cut His head.
The growth of thoughts that made me great
Lay on His cross and were its weight;
And my desires lay, turned to stone,
And where He fell, cut to the bone.
The sharpnesses of my delight
Were spikes run through His hands and feet,
And from the sweetness of my will,
Their sponge drew vinegar and gall.

Thomas Merton

STABAT MATER

By the cross her vigil keeping
Stands the queen of sorrows weeping,
  While her son in torment hangs;
Now she feels — O heart afflicted
By the sword of old predicted! —
  More than all a mother's pangs.

Who, Christ's mother contemplating
In such bitter anguish waiting,
  Has no human tears to shed ?
Who would leave Christ's mother, sharing
All the pain her son is bearing,
  By those tears uncomforted ?

Jacopone da Todi, translated by Ronald Knox

THE SEVEN VIRGINS

All under the leaves, the leaves of life,
   I met with virgins seven,
And one of them was Mary mild,
   Our Lord's mother from heaven.

'O what are you seeking, you seven fair maids,
   All under the leaves of life?
Come tell, come tell me what seek you
   All under the leaves of life.'

'We're seeking for no leaves, Thomas,
   But for a friend of thine;
We're seeking for sweet Jesus Christ,
   To be our guide and thine.'

'Go you down, go you down to yonder town
   And sit in the gallery:
And there you'll find sweet Jesus Christ
   Nailed to a big yew tree.'

So down they went to yonder town
   As fast as foot could fall,
And many a grievous bitter tear
   From the virgins' eyes did fall.

'O peace, mother, O peace, mother,
   Your weeping doth me grieve:
O I must suffer this,' he said
   'For Adam and for Eve.'

'O how can I my weeping leave,
    Or my sorrows undergo,
Whilst I do see my own son die,
    When sons I have no more ?'

'Dear mother, dear mother, you must take John
    All for to be your son,
And he will comfort you sometimes,
    Mother, as I have done.'

'O come, thou John Evangelist,
    Thou'rt welcome unto me,
But more welcome my own dear son
    That I nursed upon my knee.'

Then he laid his head on his right shoulder,
    Seeing death it struck him nigh :
'The holy ghost be with your soul —
    I die, mother dear, I die.'

O the rose, the rose, the gentle rose,
    And the fennel that grows so green !
God give us grace in every place,
    To pray for our king and queen.

                                        Anonymous

159

THE LORD LOOKS AT PETER

A night alarum, a weaponed crowd;
one blow, and with the rest I ran.
I warmed my hands, and said aloud:
I never knew the man.

John Gray

SIMON THE CYRENIAN SPEAKS

He never spoke a word to me
    And yet He called my name;
He never gave a sign to me,
    And yet I knew and came.

At first I said, 'I will not bear
    His cross upon my back,
He only seeks to place it there
    Because my skin is black.'

But He was dying for a dream,
    And He was very meek,
And in His eyes there shone a gleam
    Men journey far to seek.

It was Himself my pity bought;
    I did for Christ alone
What all of Rome could not have wrought
    With bruise of lash or stone.

Countee Cullen

160

STILL FALLS THE RAIN
The Raids, 1940. Night and Dawn

Still falls the Rain —
Dark as the world of man, black as our loss —
Blind as the nineteen hundred and forty nails
Upon the Cross.

Still falls the Rain
With a sound like the pulse of the heart that is changed to
    the hammer-beat
In the Potter's Field, and the sound of the impious feet

On the Tomb :
                Still falls the Rain
In the Field of Blood where the small hopes breed and the
    human brain
Nurtures its greed, that worm with the brow of Cain.

Still falls the Rain
At the feet of the Starved Man hung upon the Cross.
Christ that each day, each night, nails there, have mercy on
    us —
On Dives and on Lazarus :
Under the Rain the sore and the gold are as one.

Still falls the Rain —
Still falls the Blood from the Starved Man's wounded Side :
He bears in His Heart all wounds — those of the light that
    died,
The last faint spark
In the self-murdered heart, the wounds of the sad un-
    comprehending dark,
The wounds of the baited bear, —

The blind and weeping bear whom the keepers beat
On his helpless flesh . . . the tears of the hunted hare.

Still falls the Rain —
The — O Ile leape up to my God : who pulles me doune —
See, see where Christ's blood streames in the firmament :
It flows from the Brow we nailed upon the tree
Deep to the dying, to the thirsting heart
That holds the fires of the world, — dark-smirched with
    pain
As Caesar's laurel crown.

Then sounds the voice of One who like the heart of man
Was once a child who among beasts has lain —
'Still do I love, still shed my innocent light, my Blood, for
    thee.'

Edith Sitwell

DAVID'S LAMENT FOR JONATHAN

Low in thy grave with thee
        Happy to lie,
Since there's no greater thing left Love to do;
    And to live after thee
        Is but to die,
    For with but half a soul what can Life do ?

    So share thy victory
        Or else thy grave,
Either to rescue thee, or with thee lie :
    Ending that life for thee,
        That thou didst save,
    So Death that sundereth might bring more nigh.

162

Peace, O my stricken lute!
  Thy strings are sleeping.
Would that my heart could still
  Its bitter weeping!
    Peter Abelard, translated by Helen Waddell

THE FOUR EXECUTIONERS
from 'The Crucifixion'

3rd Now are we at the mount of Calvary;
Have done fellows and let's now see
  That we no sport may lack.

1st In faith, sir, since ye call yourself a king,
You must prove a worthy thing
  That wends thus to the war;
You must joust in tournament;
Unless ye sit fast ye may repent,
  By me thrust down before. . . .

3rd Thank us when thy steed thou straddle,
For we shall set thee in thy saddle,
  Fear no fall, be thou bold.
I promise no lance will shift thee,
Unless thou sit well thou had better let be
  The tales that thou hast told.

4th Stand near, fellows, and let us see
How we can horse our king so free,
  By any chance;
Stand thou yonder on that side,
And we shall see how he can ride,
  And how well wield a lance. . . .

2nd   Knit thou a knot with all thy strength,
Out to draw this arm in length,
    Till it come to the bore.

3rd   Thou madest man, by this light!
It lacks to each man's sight,
    Half a span or more.

4th   Yet draw out this arm and fix it fast,
With this rope that well will last,
    And each man lay hand to.

1st   Yea, and bind thou fast that band;
We shall go to that other hand
    And look what we can do.

2nd   Drive a nail right here throughout,
And then we need us nothing doubt
    That home it comes to rest.

3rd   That shall I do, as might I thrive!
For to clench and for to drive,
    Of all I am the best.
So let it stay for it is well.

4th   As I have bliss, the truth you tell!
    Move it no man might.

1st   Hold down his knees.

2nd   That shall I do,
Your nurse no better help gave you,
    Pull his legs down tight.

3rd Draw out his limbs much further yet.

4th That was well drawn and cost much sweat;
   Fair befall him that pulled so!
 For to have brought him to the mark
 Unlettered churl nor clerk
   More skill could show. . . .

1st I tell thee fellows, by this weather
 That we draw now altogether,
   And look how it will fare. . . .

4th Pull, pull!

1st   Have, now!

2nd   Let's see!

3rd   Ah, ha!

4th Heave ho!

1st   Now we have not far.

2nd   Hold still, I implore!

3rd So fellows! now look alive,
 Which of you now best can drive,
   And I shall take the bore.

4th Now to try my turn let me;
 Best farrier I hope to be
   For to clench it right.
 Do rouse him up now when we may,

For I hope he and his palfrey
　　Shall not part this night. . . .

3rd　Fellows, your hands now you lend,
　　For to raise this tree on end,
　　　　And let's see who is last.

4th　It is best to do as he says;
　　Set this tree in the mortice,
　　　　And there it will stand fast.

1st　Up with the timber.

2nd　　　　　　　　Ah, it holds!
　　For him that all this world upholds
　　　　Thrust from thee with thy hand!

3rd　Hold ever amongst us all.

4th　Yea, and let it in the mortice fall,
　　　　For then will it best stand.

1st　Go we to it and be we strong,
　　And raise it, be it never so long,
　　　　Since firmly we have done.

2nd　Up with the timber fast on end!

3rd　Fellows, your full force now lend!

4th　　　　So Sir, gape against the sun!

1st　Now fellow, wear thy crown!

2nd   Trust thou this timber will fall down?

3rd   Yet help that it were fast.

4th   Shake him well and let us lift.

1st   Full short be his shrift.

2nd   Ah, it stands up like a mast.

The Wakefield Cycle. Anonymous, edited by Martial Rose

GOD'S PRICE AND MAN'S PRICE

God bought man here with his heart's blood expense;
And man sold God here for base thirty pence.

Robert Herrick

THE HOLY CROSS

Christ when he died
Deceived the cross;
And on death's side
Threw all the loss.
The captive world awaked and found
The prisoner loose, the jailer bound.

Richard Crashaw

167

THE HARROWING OF HELL

Christ to hell he took the way
  With wounds wide and all bloody,
The foul fiends to affray,
  With him he bore the cross of tree.

There where the good souls did in dwell,
  They chained the gates, and barred them fast.
Ah now, said Jesus, ye princes fell,
  Open the gates that ever shall last.

Now in my father's name of heaven
  Open the gates against me!
As light of light, and thunder flame
  The gates burst and began to flee.

Ah-ha! said Adam, my God I see,
  He that made me with his hand!
I see, said Noah, whence cometh he
  That saved me both on water and land.

Quoth Beelzebub, I barred full fast
  The gates with lock, chain, bolt and pin,
And with the wind of his word's blast
  They broke up, and he came in.

Adam and Eve with him he took,
  King David, Moses and Solomon,
And harried hell in every nook.
  Within it left he souls none.

Anonymous

X

Death
and
Darkness,
get you packing

EASTER HYMN

Death and darkness, get you packing,
Nothing now to man is lacking,
All your triumphs now are ended,
And what Adam marred, is mended.

Henry Vaughan

EVERYONE SANG

Everyone suddenly burst out singing;
And I was filled with such delight
As prisoned birds must find in freedom,
Winging wildly across the white
Orchards and dark-green fields; on — on — and out of
    sight.

Everyone's voice was suddenly lifted;
And beauty came like the setting sun:
My heart was shaken with tears; and horror
Drifted away. . . . O but Every-one
Was a bird; and the song was wordless; the singing will
    never be done.

Siegfried Sassoon

THE LILY OF THE VALLEY

He's the lily of the valley,
               He's my Lord.
He's the white rose of Sharon,
               He's my Lord.

He's the great physician,
<blockquote>He's my Lord.</blockquote>
He heals your sorrows,
<blockquote>He's my Lord.</blockquote>

He's the Alpha and Omega, the beginning and the end,
<blockquote>He's my Lord.</blockquote>
He's the Shepherd of the flock, the door to enter in,
<blockquote>He's my Lord.</blockquote>

He's the Lord that was and is to come,
<blockquote>He's my Lord.</blockquote>
He's the Rock the Church is built upon,
<blockquote>He's my Lord.</blockquote>

He's the Bread of Heaven, the Truth, the Way,
<blockquote>He's my Lord.</blockquote>
He's the light that shines to a perfect day,
<blockquote>He's my Lord.</blockquote>

I'll tell the nations both great and small,
<blockquote>He's my Lord.</blockquote>
The blood of Jesus saves us all,
<blockquote>He's my Lord.</blockquote>

Anonymous. Spiritual

PRAISE TO THE HOLIEST

Praise to the holiest in the height
And in the depth be praise,
In all his words most wonderful,
Most sure in all his ways.

O loving wisdom of our God!
When all was sin and shame,
A second Adam to the fight
And to the rescue came.

O wisest love! that flesh and blood
Which did in Adam fail,
Should strive afresh against the foe,
Should strive and should prevail.

O generous love! that he who smote
In man for man the foe,
The double agony in man
For man should undergo;

And in the garden secretly,
And on the cross on high,
Should teach his brethren, and inspire
To suffer and to die.

John Henry Newman

EASTER SONG

I got me flowers to straw thy way;
I got me boughs off many a tree;
But thou wast up by break of day,
And brought'st thy sweets along with thee. . . .

Can there be any day but this,
Though many suns to shine endeavour?
We count three hundred, but we miss;
There is but one, and that one ever.

George Herbert

O FILII ET FILIAE

Ye sons and daughters of the Lord!
The king of glory, king adored,
This day himself from death restored.

All in the early morning grey
Went holy women on their way
To see the tomb where Jesus lay.

Of spices pure a precious store
In their pure hands these women bore
To anoint the sacred body o'er.

Then straightway one in white they see,
Who saith, 'Ye seek the Lord; but he
Is risen, and gone to Galilee.'

This told they Peter, told they John;
Who forthwith to the tomb are gone,
But Peter is by John outrun.

The selfsame night, while out of fear
The doors were shut, their Lord most dear
To his apostles did appear.

But Thomas, when of this he heard
Was doubtful of his brethren's word,
Wherefore again there comes the Lord.

'Thomas, behold my side,' saith he;
'My hands, my feet, my body see,
And doubt not, but believe in me.'

When Thomas saw that wounded side,
The truth no longer he denied.
'Thou art my God and Lord,' he cried.

O blest are they who have not seen
The Lord, and yet believe in him!
Eternal life awaiteth them.

Now let us praise the Lord most high
And strive his name to magnify
On this great day, through earth and sky.

Whose mercy ever runneth o'er,
Whom men and angel hosts adore,
To him be glory evermore.

Anonymous, translated by Edward Caswall

A CHINESE LYRIC

The morning glory climbs above my head,
Pale flowers of white and purple, blue and red.
      I am disquieted.

Down in the withered grasses something stirred,
I thought it was his footfall that I heard,
      Then a grasshopper chirred.

I climbed the hill just as the new moon showed,
I saw him coming on the southern road,
      My heart lays down its load.

Anonymous, translated by Helen Waddell

DOUBTING THOMAS
from 'The York Cycle'

PETER   Welcome, Thomas; where hast thou been?
Wit well, nor doubt not what I mean.
Jesus our Lord we late have seen,
         On ground to go.

THOMAS   What say ye men? Your wits, I ween,
         Are mazed for woe.

JOHN   Nay, Thomas, this is true and plain;
Jesus our Lord is risen again.

THOMAS   Away! This is the dreaming vain
         Of fools unwise.
For he that was so foully slain,
         How should he rise?
Nay, fellows; now this talk let be.
Until I shall his body see,
And lay upon his nail-prints three
         My fingers there,
And feel the wound that piercingly
         The spear did tear —
Till then, to trust no tales I mean.

JAMES   Thomas, that wound have we all seen.

THOMAS   Bah! Ye know never what ye mean;
         Your wits ye want.
Seek not — for I am not so green —
         Your tricks to plant.

JESUS   My brethren, peace to you this day.
Thomas, take tent to what I say.
Thy fingers on these wounds now lay, —
              My hands here see, —
By which for man's good did I pay,
              Nailed on a tree.

See how my wounds bleed, I command.
Here in my side put in thy hand,
And feel my wounds, and understand
              That this is I.
No more mistrust, then; feel, and stand
              In trust truly.

THOMAS   My Lord, my God! Ah, well is me!
Ah, blood of price, blest might thou be!
Mankind on earth, behold and see
              This blessed sight.
Mercy now, good Lord, ask I thee,
              With main and might.

JESUS   Thomas, because thou sawest this sight,
That I am risen by promise plight,
Thou dost believe; but every wight
              Blest be he ever
That in my rising trusts aright,
              Yet saw it never.

My brethren, fare now forth from here,
Through every land and country clear.
My rising henceforth far and near
              Preached shall be.
My blessing be on all men here,
              Who follow me.

             Anonymous, edited by J. S. Purvis

CHRIST WHOSE GLORY FILLS THE SKIES

Christ, whose glory fills the skies,
Christ, the true, the only light,
Sun of righteousness, arise,
   Triumph o'er the shades of night.
Dayspring from on high, be near;
Daystar, in my heart appear.

Charles Wesley

CANTATE DOMINO
from the Authorised Version of the Bible

O sing unto the Lord a new song; for he hath done marvellous things :

His right hand, and his holy arm, hath gotten him the victory.

The Lord hath made known his salvation : his righteousness hath he openly showed in the sight of the heathen.

He hath remembered his mercy and his truth toward the house of Israel : all the ends of the earth have seen the salvation of our God.

Make a joyful noise unto the Lord, all the earth : make a loud noise, and rejoice, and sing praise.

Sing unto the Lord with the harp; with the harp, and the voice of a psalm.

With trumpets and sound of cornet make a joyful noise before the Lord, the King.

Let the sea roar, and the fulness thereof; the world, and they that dwell therein.

Let the floods clap their hands : let the hills be joyful together before the Lord; for he cometh to judge the earth :

With righteousness shall he judge the world, and the people with equity.

Psalm 98

EASTER

Break the box and shed the nard;
Stop not now to count the cost;
Hither bring pearl, opal, sard;
Reck not what the poor have lost;
Upon Christ throw all away;
Know ye, this is Easter Day.

Build His church and deck His shrine;
Empty though it be on earth;
Ye have kept your choicest wine —
Let it flow for heavenly mirth;
Pluck the harp and breathe the horn :
Know ye not 'tis Easter morn?

Gather gladness from the skies;
Take a lesson from the ground;
Flowers do ope their heavenward eyes
And a Spring-time joy have found;
Earth throws Winter's robes away,
Decks herself for Easter Day.

Beauty now for ashes wear,
Perfumes for the garb of woe.
Chaplets for dishevelled hair,
Dances for sad footsteps slow;
Open wide your hearts that they
Let in joy this Easter Day.

Seek God's house in happy throng;
Crowded let His table be;
Mingle praises, prayer and song,
Singing to the Trinity.
Henceforth let your souls alway
Make each morn an Easter Day.

Gerard Manley Hopkins

THE FONT

Thirty generations have stood and listened
By this flowering stone,
Wondering, pondering, as their child was christened;
Would he atone
For all disasters? — their son,
Now cleansed of sin,
Attain the ambitions they never won,
Would never win?

Child after child, generation on generation
Fails and fails.
Always, it seems, the subtle degradation
Of the world prevails.
Faith drowns : soon perish
The dreams they want;
Till they stand with the hopes their fathers cherish
Beside this font. . . .

Clive Sansom

BAPTISM

from Piers Plowman, Passus XV

Cloth that comes from the weaver is not good for wearing
Until it is trod under foot or taken in the stretcher,
Washed well with water, wiped with teasels,
Tucked, and given to the tenter hooks, and to the tailor's
    finishing.
The same belongs to the babe born of woman.
Till it is christened in Christ's name and confirmed by the
    bishop
It is an heathen toward heaven, and helpless in the spirit.

Heathen is derived from *heath,* or the untilled barren.
So in the wild wilderness the wild creatures
Are rude and unreasoning and run without harness.

        William Langland, translated by H. W. Wells

CHARM

The little drop of the Father
On thy forehead, beloved one.

The little drop of the Son
On thy forehead, beloved one.

The little drop of the Spirit
On thy forehead, beloved one.

To aid thee from the fays,
To guard thee from the host.

To aid thee from the gnome,
To shield thee from the spectre.

To keep thee for the Three,
To shield thee, to surround thee.

To save thee for the Three,
To fill thee with the graces.

The little drop of the Three
To lave thee with the graces.

Anonymous. Gaelic, translated by Alexander Carmichael

THE WATERFALL

With what deep murmurs through time's silent stealth
Doth thy transparent, cool and watery wealth
      Here flowing fall
      And chide, and call,
As if his liquid, loose retinue stayed
Lingering, and were of this steep place afraid,
      The common pass
      Where, clear as glass,
      All must descend
      Not to an end :
But quickened by this deep and rocky grave,
Rise to a longer course more bright and brave.

Henry Vaughan

A FLOWER HAS OPENED

A flower has opened in my heart. . . .
What flower is this, what flower of spring,
What simple, secret thing ?
It is the peace that shines apart,
The peace of daybreak skies that bring

182

Clear song and wild swift wing.
Heart's miracle of inward light,
What powers unknown have sown your seed
And your perfection freed? . . .
O flower within me wondrous white,
I know you only as my need
And my unsealed sight.

Siegfried Sassoon

NOW THE FULL-THROATED DAFFODILS

Now the full-throated daffodils,
Our trumpeters in gold,
Call resurrection from the ground
And bid the year be bold.

Today the almond tree turns pink,
The first flush of the spring;
Winds loll and gossip through the town
Her secret whispering.

Now too the bird must try his voice
Upon the morning air;
Down drowsy avenues he cries
A novel great affair.

He tells of royalty to be;
How with her train of rose
Summer to coronation comes
Through waving wild hedgerows.

Today crowds quicken in a street,
The fish leaps in the flood:
Look there, gasometer rises,
And here bough swells to bud.

For our love's luck, our stowaway,
Stretches in his cabin;
Our youngster joy barely conceived
Shows up beneath the skin.

Our joy was but a gusty thing
Without sinew or wit,
An infant flyaway; but now
We make a man of it.

Cecil Day Lewis

MAY SONG

All on this May Day morning, together come are we,
  For the summer springs so fresh, green and gay;
We tell you of a blossoming and buds on every tree
  Drawing near unto the merry month of May.

Rise up, the master of this house, put on your chain of gold,
Be not with us offended with your name to make so bold.

Rise up the mistress of this house, with gold upon your
    breast,
And if your body be asleep, we hope your soul's at rest.

Rise up, the children of this house, put on your rich attire,
And every hair upon your head shine like a silver wire.

And now comes we must leave you in peace and plenty here,
  For the summer springs so fresh, green and gay;
We shall not sing you May again until another year,
  Drawing near unto the merry month of May.

Anonymous

THE WINTER IS PAST
from the Authorised Version of the Bible

My beloved spake, and said unto me, Rise up, my love, my fair one, and come away.

For lo, the winter is past, the rain is over and gone;

The flowers appear on the earth; the time of the singing of birds is come, and the voice of the turtle is heard in our land;

The fig tree putteth forth her green figs, and the vines with the tender grapes give a good smell. Arise, my love, my fair one, and come away.

O my dove, that art in the clefts of the rock, in the secret places of the stairs, let me see thy countenance, let me hear thy voice; for sweet is thy voice, and thy countenance is comely.

Take us the foxes, the little foxes, that spoil the vines : for our vines have tender grapes.

My beloved is mine, and I am his : he feedeth among the lilies.

Until the day break, and the shadows flee away, turn, my beloved, and be thou like a roe or a young hart upon the mountains of Bether.

Song of Solomon

THE SEVEN JOYS

The first good joy that Mary had,
It was the joy of one,
To see the blessed Jesus Christ,
When he was first her son.

When he was first her son, good man,
And blessed may he be,
Both Father, Son, and Holy Ghost,
Through all Eternity.

The next good joy that Mary had,
It was the joy of two,
To see her own son, Jesus Christ,
To make the lame to go.

The next good joy that Mary had,
It was the joy of three,
To see her own son, Jesus Christ,
To make the blind to see.

The next good joy that Mary had,
It was the joy of four,
To see her own son, Jesus Christ,
To read the Bible o'er.

The next good joy that Mary had,
It was the joy of five,
To see her own son, Jesus Christ,
To bring the dead alive.

The next good joy that Mary had,
It was the joy of six,
To see her own son, Jesus Christ,
Upon the crucifix.

The next good joy that Mary had,
It was the joy of seven,
To see her own son, Jesus Christ,
To wear the crown of heaven.

> *To wear the crown of heaven, good man,*
> *And blessed may he be,*
> *Both Father, Son, and Holy Ghost,*
> *Through all eternity.*

Anonymous

WHAT IS HE THAT COMES?

What is he, this lordling, that cometh from the fight,
With blood-red tunic so terribly bedight?
So fairly armed, so seemly in sight,
So sturdily marching, so doughty a knight?

I am he, I am he who speaks nothing but right,
The champion to stand for mankind in the fight.
William Herebert

THE ASCENSION

Lift up your heads, great gates, and sing,
Now glory comes, and glory's king;
Now by your high all-golden way
The fairer heaven comes home today.
Hark! now the gates are ope, and hear
The tune of each triumphant sphere;
Where every Angel, as he sings,
Keeps time with his applauding wings,
And makes heaven's loftiest roof rebound
The echoes of the noble sound.

Joseph Beaumont

WHO WILL BE THE DRIVER?

O who will be the driver when the bridegroom comes?
O who will be the driver when he comes?
O who will be the driver? O who will be the driver?
O who will be the driver when he comes?

187

King David'll be the driver when the bridegroom comes.

He'll be driving six white horses when the bridegroom
comes. . . .

O who will go to meet him when the bridegroom comes?

We'll all go forth to meet him when the bridegroom comes.
We'll all go forth to meet him when he comes.
We'll all go forth to meet him, we'll all go forth to meet
him,
We'll all go forth to meet him when he comes.

Anonymous

TO THE SUN

O let your shining orb grow dim,
Of Christ the mirror and the shield,
That I may gaze through you to Him,
See half the miracle revealed,
And in your seven hues behold
The Blue Man walking on the sea;
The Green, beneath the summer tree,
Who called the children; then the Gold,
With palms; the Orange, flaring bold
With scourges; Purple in the garden
(As Greco saw): and then the Red
Torero (Him who took the toss
And rode the black horns of the cross —
But rose snow-silver from the dead!)

Roy Campbell

The Spirit
is running,
the Darkness
is ending

XI

THE SPIRIT DANCES

They shall all come and you too shall come,
My people shall come and Hell shall be harrowed.
I touch you, I touch you, the spirit is running
To you and through you, the tongues are descending,
You cannot escape them, and No shall be Yes and
Yes shall be No and Hell shall be harrowed.
And Hell shall be harrowed, I touch you, I touch you
And through you and to you I weave in between you;
The blind are the seeing, the lame are the dancing
And light is ascending,
The Spirit is running, the Darkness is ending.
Light and we turn in you, peace and we burn in you
This is the Harrowing.

Thomas Blackburn

VENI CREATOR

Come Holy Ghost, Creator, come,
And with your servants live,
To hearts that you yourself have made
Your grace from heaven give.

We name you as our strengthener,
God's gift from out his height,
Love's-self and fire and source of life,
Soul's-hardening for the fight.

God's finger writing in our hearts,
Yourself seven times a gift,
The father's solemn promise, you
With words our tongues enriched.

A flame to guide our senses, light
With love our hearts endower,
The failings of our flesh supply
With never-failing power.

Still further yet drive back our foe
And straightway give your peace,
With you before us leading on
May we from all harm cease.

Through you may we the Father know,
And learn through you the Son,
Have faith in you for ever more,
Of both the Spirit one.

All glory to the Father be,
And to the risen Son,
All glory Holy Ghost to you
While endless ages run.

Anonymous, translated by Brian Moore

From 'Little Gidding', Part IV

The dove descending breaks the air
With flame of incandescent terror
Of which the tongues declare
The one discharge from sin and error.
The only hope, or else despair
      Lies in the choice of pyre or pyre —
      To be redeemed from fire by fire.

Who then devised the torment? Love.
Love is the unfamiliar Name
Behind the hands that wove

192

The intolerable shirt of flame
Which human power cannot remove.
We only live, only suspire
Consumed by either fire or fire.

T. S. Eliot

TRINITY
from 'Piers Plowman', Passus XVII

The Father was first like a fist with fingers folded,
Till at his love and liking he unloosed his fingers
And proffered his palm to the place that he favoured.
That palm is plainly the hand which proffers the fingers
To make and to minister what the might of the hand wishes.
And truly it betokens, as you may tell at pleasure,
The Holy Ghost of Heaven; he is the palm.
The fingers that are free to fold and fashion
Signify the Son, who was sent among us.
The palm taught him to touch and try his mother,
The maiden, Saint Mary, and snatch man's salvation. . . .

The Father is a fist with fingers for handling . . .
Whatever the palm perceives profitable to deal with.
They are all one, in a hand's likeness,
Which may be seen as single or in three separate natures.
Since the palm puts forth to us both fist and fingers,
We see how reason will readily recognize it,
And the Sire and the Son show it to the Spirit.

The hand holds hard all that is within it,
Through four fingers and the thumb and the force of the palm.
So the Sire and the Son and *Spiritus Sanctus*
Hold the whole wide world within them,
Air and wind and earth and water,
Heaven and hell and all that is within them. . . .

As my fist is a full hand folded together,
So the Father is the full deity, the former and creator,
And his might makes all that is made ever.

The full hand is formed with fingers; for painting and
     drawing
Carving and cutting are all crafts of the fingers.
And so is the Son the science of the Father,
A full Deity as the Father, neither feebler nor stronger.

The palm is properly the hand, and has powers independent
Of the firm fist and the fingers' workmanship.
The palm has power to place joints outward
And to fold and unfold the fist, for this is its function.
It may receive or refuse what is reached it by the fingers
After it has felt what the fist and fingers give it.
So God the Holy Ghost is neither greater nor lesser
Than the Sire or the Son, but has the same power :
And all but one God, as my hand and fingers,
Folded or unfolded, fist or palmwise, —
All is but one hand, however I turn it.

                    William Langland, translated by H. W. Wells

THE THEOLOGY OF BONGWI, THE BABOON

       This is the wisdom of the Ape
           Who yelps beneath the Moon —
       'Tis God who made me in His shape,
           He is a Great Baboon.
       'Tis He who tilts the moon askew
           And fans the forest trees,
       The heavens which are broad and blue
           Provide Him His trapeze;
       He swings with tail divinely bent

Around those azure bars
And munches to His Soul's content
   The kernels of the stars;
And when I die, His loving care
   Will raise me from the sod
To learn the perfect Mischief there,
   The Nimbleness of God.

Roy Campbell

HEAVEN

Fish (fly-replete, in depth of June,
Dawdling away their wat'ry noon)
Ponder deep wisdom, dark or clear,
Each secret fishy hope or fear.
Fish say, they have their Stream and Pond;
But is there anything Beyond?
This life cannot be All, they swear,
For how unpleasant, if it were!
One may not doubt that, somehow, Good
Shall come of Water and of Mud;
And sure, the reverent eye must see
A purpose in Liquidity.
We darkly know, by Faith we cry,
The future is not Wholly Dry.
Mud unto mud! — Death eddies near —
Not here the appointed End, not here!
But somewhere, beyond Space and Time,
Is wetter water, slimier slime!
And there (they trust) there swimmeth One
Who swam ere rivers were begun,
Immense, of fishy form and mind,
Squamous, omnipotent, and kind;
And under that Almighty Fin,

The littlest fish may enter in.
Oh! never fly conceals a hook,
Fish say, in the Eternal Brook,
But more than mundane weeds are there,
And mud, celestially fair;
Fat caterpillars drift around,
And Paradisal grubs are found;
Unfading moths, immortal flies,
And the worm that never dies.
And in that Heaven of all their wish,
There shall be no more land, say fish.

Rupert Brooke

THE YOUNG MAN

There is a young man,
who lives in a world of progress.
He used to worship a God
who was kind to him.
This God had a long white beard,
He lived in the clouds,
but all the same
He was close to the solemn child
who had secretly
shut Him up, in a picture book.

But now,
the man is enlightened.

Now he has been to school,
and has learnt to kick a ball,
and to be abject
in the face of public opinion.
He knows too,
that men are hardly removed from monkeys.
You see, he lives in the light
of the twentieth century.

He works, twelve hours a day,
and is able to rent a room,
in a lodging house,
that is not a home.
At night he hangs
a wretched coat
up on a peg on the door,
and stares
at the awful jug and basin,
and goes to bed.
And the poor coat,
worn to the man's shape,
round-shouldered and abject,
watches him, asleep,
dreaming of all
the essential
holy things,
that he cannot hope to obtain
for two pounds ten a week.

Very soon
he will put off his body,
like the poor dejected coat
that he hates.

And his body will be
worn to the shape
of twelve hours' work a day
for two pounds ten a week.

If he had only known
that the God in the picture book,
is not an old man in the clouds
but the seed of life in his soul,
the man would have lived.
And his life would have flowered
with the flower of limitless joy.

But he does not know,
and in him
the Holy Ghost
is a poor little bird
in a cage,
who never sings,
and never opens his wings,
yet never, never
desires to be gone away.

Caryll Houselander

GOD'S GIFT

Gift better than himself God doth not know,
   Gift better than his God no man can see;
This gift doth here the giver given bestow,
   Gift to this gift let each receiver be :
God is my gift, himself he freely gave me,
God's gift am I, and none but God shall have me.

Robert Southwell

GODHEAD HERE IN HIDING

Godhead here in hiding, whom I do adore
Masked by these bare shadows, shape and nothing more,
See, Lord, at thy service low lies here a heart
Lost, all lost in wonder at the God thou art.

Seeing, touching, tasting are in thee deceived;
How says trusty hearing? that shall be believed;
What God's Son has told me, take for truth I do;
Truth himself speaks truly or there's nothing true.

On the cross thy Godhead made no sign to men;
Here thy very manhood steals from human ken:
Both are my confession, both are my belief,
And I pray the prayer of the dying thief.

I am not like Thomas, wounds I cannot see,
But can plainly call thee Lord and God as he:
This faith each day deeper be my holding of,
Daily make me harder hope and dearer love.

O thou our reminder of Christ crucified,
Living Bread the life of us for whom he died,
Lend this life to me then: feed and feast my mind,
There be thou the sweetness man was meant to find. . . .

Jesu whom I look at shrouded here below,
I beseech thee send me what I thirst for so,
Some day to gaze on thee face to face in light
And be blest for ever with thy glory's sight.

Gerard Manley Hopkins

THE FALCON

Lully, lulley! Lully, lulley!
The falcon has borne my mate away.

> He bare him up, he bare him down,
> He bare him into an orchard brown.

> In that orchard there was a hall
> That was hanged with purple and pall.

> In that hall there was a bed,
> It was hanged with gold so red.

> And in that bed there lies a knight,
> His wounds bleeding day and night.

> At that bed's foot there lies a hound,
> Licking the blood as it runs down.

> By that bed-side there kneels a may,
> And she weeps both night and day.

> And at that bed's head stands a stone,
> *Corpus Christi* written thereon.

Lully, lulley! Lully, lulley!
The falcon has borne my mate away.

Anonymous

VENI SANCTE SPIRITUS

> Holy Spirit, God of Love
> Come, and let fall from above
>> Ray of your light.

Father, come to those in need,
Come rewarding every deed,
Light of our hearts.

You the one who best consoles,
You most welcome guest of souls,
Refuge and rest.

Respite in the toil of life,
Subduer of the passions' strife,
Comfort in grief.

Light that blessedness imparts,
Fill the inmost core of hearts
Faithful and true.

In your absence all is pain,
Man's endeavour all in vain,
Harmful all things.

What is soiled wash again,
What is arid bless with rain,
What wounded, heal.

Warm again the love grown cold,
What unyielding, shape and mould,
What wayward, rule.

Give to faithful hearts confessing
Gifts beyond all else possessing
Seven-fold worth.

Crown the strivings of the soul,
Give, when we have reached the goal,
Joy evermore.

Anonymous, translated by Brian Moore

LO HERE IS FELLOWSHIP

Lo, here is fellowship,
One faith to hold,
One truth to speak,
One wrong to wreak,
   One loving-cup to sip,
       And to dip
   In one dish faithfully,
      As lambkins of one fold.
Either for other to suffer all thing.
     One song to sing
In sweet accord and maken melody.
Right-so thou and I good-fellows be :
     Now God us save.

Anonymous

DIVERUS AND LAZARUS

As it fell out upon one day
   Rich Diverus made a feast,
And he invited all his friends
   And gentry of the best.

As it fell out upon one day,
   Lazarus he was so poor,
He came and laid him down and down,
   And down at Diverus' door.

So Lazarus laid him down and down,
   And down at Diverus' door :
'Some meat, some drink, brother Diverus,
   Do bestow upon the poor.'

'Thou art none of my brother, Lazarus,
    That lies begging at my door;
No meat nor drink will I give thee,
    Or bestow upon the poor.'

Then Lazarus laid him down and down
    And down at Diverus' gate :
'Some meat, some drink, Brother Diverus,
    For Jesus Christ his sake.'

'Thou art none of my brother, Lazarus,
    That lies begging at my gate,
No meat nor drink will I give thee
    For Jesus Christ his sake.'

Then Lazarus laid him down and down
    And down at Diverus' wall :
'Some meat, some drink, brother Diverus,
    Or with hunger starve I shall.'

'Thou art none of my brother, Lazarus,
    That lies begging at my wall :
No meat nor drink will I give thee,
    But with hunger starve you shall.'. . .

Then Diverus sent out his hungry dogs
    To bite him as he lay;
They had no power to bite one bite,
    But licked his sores away.

As it fell out upon a day,
    Poor Lazarus sickened and died;
There came two angels out of heaven,
    His soul therein to guide.

'Rise up, rise up, brother Lazarus,
  And come along with me,
For you've a place in heaven prepared,
  To sit on an angel's knee.'

As it fell out upon a day,
  Rich Diverus sickened and died;
There came two serpents out of Hell
  His soul therein to guide.

'Rise up, rise up, Brother Diverus,
  And go with us to see
A dismal place prepared in hell,
  To sit on a serpent's knee.'

Anonymous

THE SUN THAT WARMS YOU

Is it not so, brother?
        The sun that warms you
                              warms me,
        The fate that forms me
                              forms you,
        The irk that frets you
                              frets me,
        The rain that wets me
                              wets you,
        The hour that tries you
                              tries me,
        But the sun that dries me
                              dries you.
It is so, brother.

Eleanor Farjeon

204

LOVE THE SAMARITAN
from 'Piers Plowman', Passus XVII

As we went on the way talking together
We saw a Samaritan sitting in his saddle,
Riding rapidly on the road that we had taken,
Coming from a country that men call Jericho,
And hastening on his way to a joust in Jerusalem.
He overtook the herald and Hope together,
Where a man was wounded and waylaid by robbers.
He could neither stand nor stir nor signal for assistance,
Nor in any way save himself, and seemed half perished, —
Naked as a needle and no help about him.

Faith had first sight of him, but veered around him,
And would not come near him by nine furrows.

Hope came hastening after. He had already boasted
How he had helped many men with Moses' covenant.
But when he saw that sight he stepped sidewise
As much in dread, by this day, as a duck of a falcon!

But as soon as the Samaritan saw the sick man
He alighted from his horse and led him by the bridle,
And went to that wanderer, found his wounds open,
And perceived by his pulse that he was at the point of dying;
That unless a saviour came speedily he should not rise
     living.
He unbuckled his two bottles and poured both together,
He washed his wounds with wine and oil,
Anointed him and bound his head and carried him carefully
And held him upon his horse till they arrived at *Lex Christi*,
An inn six or seven miles this side the New Market.

He harboured him in the hostelry and called the host to him
And said : 'Here, keep this man till I come from the jousting ;
Look, here is silver,' he said, 'for salve for his injuries.'
He provided two pennies to pay for his nourishment,
And said, 'If he spends further, I shall make good hereafter
For I may not stay,' he said ; and bestrode his charger,
And so rode rapidly on the highroad to Jerusalem.

William Langland, translated by H. W. Wells

ON THE SWAG

His body doubled
under the pack
that sprawls untidily
on his old back,
the cold wet deadbeat
plods up the track.

The cook peers out :
'O curse that old lag
here again
with his clumsy swag
made of a dirty
old turnip bag.'

'Bring him in cook
from the gray level sleet
put silk on his body
slippers on his feet,
give him fire
and bread and meat.

'Let the fruit be plucked
and the cake be iced,
the bed be snug
and the wine be spiced
in the old cove's nightcap:
for this is Christ.'

R. A. K. Mason

CHARITY
from the Authorised Version of the Bible

Though I speak with the tongues of men and of angels, and
have not charity, I am become as sounding brass, or a
tinkling cymbal.

And though I have the gift of prophecy, and understand all
mysteries, and all knowledge; and though I have all
faith, so that I could remove mountains, and have not
charity, I am nothing.

And though I bestow all my goods to feed the poor, and
though I give my body to be burned, and have not
charity, it profiteth me nothing.

Charity suffereth long, and is kind; charity envieth not;
charity vaunteth not itself, is not puffed up,

Doth not behave itself unseemly, seeketh not her own, is
not easily provoked, thinketh no evil;

Rejoiceth not in iniquity, but rejoiceth in the truth;

Beareth all things, believeth all things, hopeth all things,
endureth all things.

Charity never faileth.

St. Paul: First Epistle to the Corinthians, Chapter XIII

PRAYER
from 'The Passing of Arthur'

If thou shouldst never see my face again
Pray for my soul. More things are wrought by prayer
Than this world dreams of. Wherefore, let thy voice
Rise like a fountain for me night and day.
For what are men better than sheep or goats
That nourish a blind life within the brain,
If, knowing God, they lift not hands of prayer
Both for themselves and those who call them friend?
For so the whole round earth is every way
Bound by gold chains about the feet of God.

Alfred Lord Tennyson

GOD BE IN MY HEAD

God be in my head,
   And in my understanding.
God be in mine eyes,
   And in my looking;
God be in my mouth,
   And in my speaking;
God be in my heart,
   And in my thinking;
God be at my end
   And at my departing.

Anonymous

XII

And
the City
was
pure gold

PLEASURE IT IS

Pleasure it is
To hear, I wis,
The birdes sing.
The deer in the dale,
The sheep in the vale,
The corn springing.

God's purveyance
For sustenance
It is for man.
Then we always
To give him praise
And thank him then.

William Cornish

THE HOCK-CART

Come, sons of summer, by whose toil,
We are the lords of wine and oil :
By whose tough labours, and rough hands,
We rip up first, then reap our lands.
Crowned with the ears of corn, now come,
And, to the pipe, sing harvest home. . . .
About the cart, hear, how the rout
Of rural younglings raise the shout;
Pressing before, some coming after,
Those with a shout, and these with laughter.
Some bless the cart, some kiss the sheaves;
Some prank them up with oaken leaves;
Some cross the fill-horse; some with great
Devotion, stroke the home-borne wheat :
While other rustics, less attent

211

To prayers, than to merriment,
Run after with their breeches rent. . . .

Robert Herrick

LIBRA

The gold scales of heaven
See how they swing
With fruits of the fall
That were flowers in the spring.

Fill the gold scales
With apples and pears,
Seraphim, Cherubim,
Come for your shares.

Weigh the gold scales
With damson and plum,
Come, saints and angels
And archangels, come.

Eleanor Farjeon

WHAT WILT THOU OFFER?

On the day when death will knock at thy door what wilt
    thou offer to him?
Oh, I will set before my guest the full vessel of my life —
    I will never let him go with empty hands.
All the sweet vintage of all my autumn days and summer
    nights, all the earnings and gleanings of my busy life
    will I place before him at the close of my days when
    death will knock at my door.

Rabindranath Tagore

BEFORE SLEEP

The toil of day is ebbing,
    The quiet comes again,
In slumber deep relaxing
    The limbs of tired men.

And minds with anguish shaken,
    And spirits racked with grief,
The cup of all forgetting
    Have drunk and found relief.

The still Lethean waters
    Now steal through every vein,
And men no more remember
    The meaning of their pain. . . .

Lo, let the weary body
    Lie sunk in slumber deep.
The heart shall still remember
    Christ in its very sleep.

Prudentius, translated by Helen Waddell

THE LORD IS MY SHEPHERD
from the Authorised Version of the Bible

The Lord is my shepherd; I shall not want.

He maketh me to lie down in green pastures : he leadeth me beside still waters.

He restoreth my soul : he leadeth me in the paths of righteousness for his name's sake.

Yea, though I walk through the valley of the shadow of death, I will fear no evil : for thou art with me; thy rod and thy staff they comfort me.

Psalm 23

DAY OF THE DEAD

Along the avenue of cypresses,
All in their scarlet cloaks and surplices
Of linen, go the chanting choristers,
The priests in gold and black, the villagers. . . .

And all along the path to the cemetery
The round dark heads of men crowd silently,
And black-scarved faces of women-folk, wistfully
Watch at the banner of death, and the mystery.

And at the foot of a grave a father stands
With sunken head; and forgotten, folded hands;
And at the foot of a grave a mother kneels
With pale shut face, nor either hears nor feels

The coming of the chanting choristers
Between the avenue of cypresses,
The silence of the many villagers,
The candle-flames beside the surplices.

D. H. Lawrence

IN TIME OF PESTILENCE

Rich men, trust not in wealth,
Gold cannot buy you health;
Physic himself must fade,
All things to end are made.
The plague full swift goes by.
I am sick, I must die.
    Lord have mercy on us!

Beauty is but a flower
Which wrinkles will devour;

214

Brightness falls from the air,
Queens have died young and fair,
Dust hath closed Helen's eye.
I am sick, I must die.
Lord have mercy on us!

Thomas Nashe

DEATH BE NOT PROUD

Death be not proud, though some have called thee
Mighty and dreadful, for thou art not so,
For those whom thou thinkest thou dost overthrow,
Die not, poor death; nor yet canst thou kill me.
From rest and sleep, which but thy pictures be,
Much pleasure, then from thee, much more must flow,
And soonest our best men with thee do go,
Rest of their bones and souls' delivery!
Thou art slave to Fate, Chance, kings, and desperate men,
And dost with poison, war, and sickness dwell,
And poppy, or charms can make us sleep as well
And better than thy stroke. Why swellest thou then?
One short sleep past, we wake eternally,
And death shall be no more: death, thou shalt die!

John Donne

ONE O' THESE MORNIN'S

One o' these mornin's bright an' fair,
Gwine to hitch on my wings an' try the air.

When I gets to heaven, got nothin' to do
But fly around and sing hallelu.

215

Away up in heaven where I'm gwine to shout
Nobody dare to put me out.

I haven' been to heaven, but I been tol'
The streets in heaven are paved in gol'.

I want to go to heaven at my own expense,
If I cain' get through the gate, I'll jump the fence.

When I get to heaven I want to go right,
I want to go to heaven all dressed in white.

When I get to heaven, gwine to take my stan',
Gwine to wrastle with my Lord like a natural man.

When I get to heaven, gwine to sit an' tell,
Tell them angels to ring them bells.

When I get to heaven, gwine to be at my ease,
Me an' my God's gwine to do as we please.

Anonymous

THE TIRED WOMAN

Here lies a poor woman who was always tired,
She lived in a house where help was not hired.
Her last words on earth were: 'Dear friends, I am going
Where washing ain't done, nor sweeping, nor sewing;
But everything there is exact to my wishes;
For where they don't eat there's no washing of dishes.
I'll be where loud anthems will always be ringing,
But having no voice I'll be clear of the singing.
Don't mourn for me now, don't mourn for me never —
I'm going to do nothing for ever and ever.'

Anonymous

216

A VISION OF GOD
from the Authorised Version of the Bible

After this I looked, and behold, a door was opened in heaven: and the first voice which I heard was as it were of a trumpet talking with me; which said, Come up hither, and I will show thee things which must be hereafter.

And immediately I was in the spirit: and behold a throne was set in heaven, and one sat on the throne.

And he that sat was to look upon like a jasper and a sardine stone: and there was a rainbow round about the throne, in sight like unto an emerald.

And round about the throne were four and twenty seats: and upon the seats I saw four and twenty elders sitting, clothed in white raiment; and they had on their heads crowns of gold.

And out of the throne proceeded lightnings and thunderings and voices: and there were seven lamps of fire burning before the throne, which are the seven Spirits of God.

And before the throne there was a sea of glass like unto crystal: and in the midst of the throne, and round about the throne, were four beasts full of eyes before and behind.

And the first beast was like a lion, and the second beast was like a calf, and the third beast had a face as a man, and the fourth beast was like a flying eagle.

And the four beasts had each of them six wings about him; and they were full of eyes within: and they rest not day and night, saying, Holy, holy, holy, Lord God Almighty, which was, and is, and is to come.

St. John: Revelation, Chapter IV

IS THERE ANY REWARD?

Is there any reward?
I'm beginning to doubt it.
I am broken and bored,
Is there any reward?
Reassure me, good Lord,
And inform me about it.
Is there any reward?
I'm beginning to doubt it.

Hilaire Belloc

EXTREME UNCTION

Upon the eyes, the lips, the feet,
On all the passages of sense,
The atoning oil is spread with sweet
Renewal of lost innocence.

The feet, that lately ran so fast
To meet desire, are soothly sealed;
The eyes that were so often cast
On vanity, are touched and healed.

From troublous sights and sounds set free;
In such a twilight hour of breath,
Shall one retrace his life, or see
Through shadows, the true face of death?

Vials of mercy! sacring oils!
I know not where nor when I come,
Nor through what wanderings and toils,
To crave of you Viaticum.

218

Yet, when the walls of flesh grow weak,
  In such an hour, it well may be,
Through mist and darkness, light will break,
  And each anointed sense will see.

Ernest Dowson

EVEN SUCH IS TIME

Even such is Time, which takes in trust
Our youth, our joys, our all we have,
And pays us but with age and dust,
Who in the dark and silent grave,
When we have wandered all our ways
Shuts up the story of our days.
And from which earth, and grave, and dust,
The Lord shall raise me up I trust.

Walter Raleigh

THE LYKE-WAKE DIRGE

This ae night, this ae night,
  Every night and all,
Fire and fleet and candle-light,
  And Christ receive thy soul.

When thou from hence away art past,
  Every night and all,
To Whinny-muir thou comest at last,
  And Christ receive thy soul.

If ever thou gavest hosen and shoon,
  Every night and all,
Sit thee down and put them on,
  And Christ receive thy soul.

If hosen and shoon thou never gavest none,
Every night and all,
The whins shall prick thee to the bare bone,
And Christ receive thy soul.

From Whinny-muir when thou mayest pass,
Every night and all,
To Brig o' Dread thou comest at last,
And Christ receive thy soul.

From Brig o' Dread when thou mayest pass,
Every night and all,
To Purgatory fire thou comest at last,
And Christ receive thy soul.

If ever thou gavest meat or drink,
Every night and all,
The fire shall never make thee shrink,
And Christ receive thy soul.

If meat or drink thou never gavest none,
Every night and all,
The fire shall burn thee to the bare bone,
And Christ receive thy soul.

This ae night, this ae night,
Every night and all,
Fire and fleet and candle-light,
And Christ receive thy soul.

Anonymous

220

THE DAY OF JUDGMENT

O day of life, of light, of love!
The only day dealt from above!
A day so fresh, so bright, so brave
Twill show us each forgotten grave,
And make the dead, like flowers, arise
Youthful and fair to see new skies.

Henry Vaughan

GENERAL WILLIAM BOOTH
ENTERS INTO HEAVEN

Booth led boldly with his big brass drum —
(*Are you washed in the blood of the Lamb?*)
The saints smiled gravely and they said : 'He's come.'
(*Are you washed in the blood of the Lamb?*)
Walking lepers followed, rank on rank,
Lurching bravos from the ditches dank,
Drabs from the alleyways and drug fiends pale —
Minds still passion-ridden, soul-powers frail : —
Vermin-eaten saints with moldy breath,
Unwashed legions with the ways of Death —
(*Are you washed in the blood of the Lamb?*)

Every slum had sent its half-a-score
The round world over. (Booth had groaned for more.)
Every banner that the wide world flies
Bloomed with glory and transcendent dyes.
Big-voiced lasses made their banjos bang,
Tranced, fanatical they shrieked and sang : —
'Are you washed in the blood of the Lamb ?'
Hallelujah! It was queer to see
Bull-necked convicts with that land make free.
Loons with trumpets blowed a blare, blare, blare

On, on upward thro' the golden air!
(*Are you washed in the blood of the Lamb?*)

Booth died blind and still by faith he trod,
Eyes still dazzled by the ways of God.
Booth led boldly, and he looked the chief,
Eagle countenance in sharp relief,
Beard a-flying, air of high command
Unabated in that holy land.

Jesus came from out the court-house door,
Stretched his hands above the passing poor.
Booth saw not, but led his queer ones there
Round and round the mighty court-house square.
Then, in an instant all that blear review
Marched on spotless, clad in raiment new.
The lame were straightened, withered limbs uncurled
And blind eyes opened on a new, sweet world.

Drabs and vixens in a flash made whole!
Gone was the weasel-head, the snout, the jowl!
Sages and sibyls now, and athletes clean,
Rulers of empires, and of forests green!
The hosts were sandalled, and their wings were fire!
(*Are you washed in the blood of the Lamb?*)
But their noise played havoc with the angel-choir.
(*Are you washed in the blood of the Lamb?*)
O shout Salvation! It was good to see
Kings and Princes by the Lamb set free.
The banjos rattled and the tambourines
Jing-jing-jingled in the hands of Queens.

And when Booth halted by the curb for prayer
He saw his Master thro' the flag-filled air.

222

Christ came gently with a robe and crown
For Booth the soldier, while the throng knelt down.
He saw King Jesus. They were face to face,
And he knelt a-weeping in that holy place.
(Are you washed in the blood of the Lamb?)

Vachel Lindsay

WHO HAS NOT FOUND
THE HEAVEN BELOW

Who has not found the heaven below
    Will fail of it above —
For angels rent the house next ours
    Whenever we remove.

Emily Dickinson

MY SOUL THERE IS A COUNTRY

My soul there is a country
    Far beyond the stars,
Where stands a winged sentry
    All skilful in the wars,
There above noise, and danger
    Sweet Peace sits crowned with smiles,
And one born in a manger
    Commands the beauteous files.
He is thy gracious friend,
    And (O my soul awake!)
Did in pure love descend
    To die here for thy sake.
If thou canst get but thither

223

There grows the flower of Peace,
   The rose that cannot wither,
      Thy fortress, and thy ease.
Leave then thy foolish ranges;
   For none can thee secure,
      But one, who never changes,
   Thy God, thy life, thy cure.

Henry Vaughan

JERUSALEM : A PRISONER'S SONG

Jerusalem, thy joys divine —
   No joys may be compared to them;
No people blessed so are thine,
   No city like Jerusalem. . . .

The trees do blossom, bud and bear,
   The birds do ever chirp and sing,
The fruit is mellow all the year,
   They have an everlasting spring;
The pleasant gardens ever keep
   Their herbs and flowers fresh and green,
All sorts of pleasant dainty fruits
   At all times there are to be seen.

The lily white, the ruddy rose,
   The crimson and carnation flowers,
Be watered there with honey dews
   And heavenly drops of golden showers.
Pomegranates (prince of fruit), the peach,
   The dainty date and pleasant fig,
The almond, muscatel and grape,
   Exceeding good and wondrous big.

224

The lemon, orange medlar, quince,
    The apricot and Indian spice,
The cherry, warden plum and pear —
    More sorts than were in Paradise —
The fruits more eisome, toothsome, fair
    Than that which grew on Adam's tree;
For whose delights assailed were
    And both suppressed Eve and he . . .

The river wine most pleasant flows,
    More pleasant than the honey comb,
Upon whose banks the sugar grows,
    Enclosed in reeds of cinnamon.

Anonymous

THROUGH THE STRAIT PASS OF SUFFERING

Through the strait pass of suffering
The martyrs even trod,
Their feet upon temptation,
Their faces upon God.

A stately, shriven company,
Convulsion playing round
Harmless as streaks of meteor
Upon a planet's bond.

Their faith the everlasting truth
Their expectation fair,
The needle to the north degree
Wades so through polar air.

Emily Dickinson

Therefore come they, the crowding maidens,
Gertrude, Agnes, Prisca, Cecily,
Lucy, Thecla, Juliana,
    Barbara, Agatha, Petronel.

And other maids whose names I have read not,
Names I have read and now record not,
But their soul and their faith were maimed not,
    Worthy now of God's company.

Wandering through the fresh fields go they,
Gathering flowers to make them a nosegay,
Gathering roses red for the Passion,
    Lilies and violets for love.

Sigebert of Gembloux, translated by Helen Waddell

CITY OF GOD

from the Authorised Version of the Bible

And the building of the wall of it was of jasper: and the
city was pure gold, like unto clear glass.

And the foundations of the wall of the city were garnished
with all manner of precious stones. The first founda-
tion was jasper; the second, sapphire; the third, a
chalcedony; the fourth, an emerald;

The fifth, sardonyx; the sixth, sardius; the seventh,
chrysolyte; the eighth, beryl; the ninth, a topaz; the
tenth, a chrysoprasus; the eleventh, a jacinth; the
twelfth, an amethyst.

And the twelve gates were twelve pearls; every several
gate was of one pearl: and the street of the city was

pure gold, as it were transparent glass.

And I saw no temple therein : for the Lord God Almighty
and the Lamb are the temple of it.

And the city had no need of the sun, neither of the moon, to
shine in it : for the glory of God did lighten it, and the
Lamb is the light thereof.

St. John: Revelation, Chapter XXI

THE GOLDEN JOURNEY TO SAMARKAND

We are the Pilgrims, master; we shall go
　　Always a little further : it may be
Beyond that last blue mountain barred with snow,
　　Across that angry or that glimmering sea,

White on a throne or guarded in a cave
　　There lives a prophet who can understand
Why men were born : but surely we are brave,
　　Who make the golden journey to Samarkand.

James Elroy Flecker

Index of Authors

Index of First Lines

231

PRINTED IN GREAT BRITAIN BY ROBERT MACLEHOSE AND CO. LTD
THE UNIVERSITY PRESS, GLASGOW